PRAISE FOR
Parenting Out of the Box

How refreshing, a parenting book that breaks the mold! *Parenting Out of the Box* teaches parents how to tap into their child's self-esteem to help them grow up to be independent, resilient adults! With honesty, compassion and tons of humor that leaves you laughing out loud, Pamela J. Bolen shows you how to effectively connect with your kids and teens.

— TRACEY MITCHELL, AUTHOR OF DOWNSIDE UP, TRANSFORM REJECTION INTO YOUR GOLDEN OPPORTUNITY

Parenting Out of the Box delivers an arsenal of practical tools to support parents as they seek to raise healthy, confident, and independent children and teens. Written by an experienced family counselor who provides a wealth of wisdom, the author equips parents with skills to succeed. Pamela J. Bolen's engaging writing and transparency empowers parents and her humor provides encouragement. Join fun in the toy box as you let old childhood friends become metaphors to teach healthy skills in self-esteem. What better way to learn than to laugh along the way!

— JODY CAPEHART, CO-AUTHOR BONDING WITH YOUR TEEN THROUGH BOUNDARIES EDUCATOR, SCHOOL ADMINISTRATOR, AUTHOR OF MANY PARENTING BOOKS

In a world filled with entitlement issues, Pamela J. Bolen's book, *Parenting Out of the Box,* is a light for parents, grandparents, and caretakers. If you've ever wondered how to support your child's self-esteem without raising their expectation for entitlement, this book is a must read! The author, both a parent and therapist, unravels the web of confusion and gives solid, profound suggestions for growing happy children into responsible adults.

— MELANIE HEMRY, AUTHOR *A HEALING TOUCH: THE POWER OF PRAYER*

Parenting Out of the Box is a must read for parents! Parents have such an essential role in the development of their children's self-esteem. Yet many parents feel they themselves are ill-equipped to influence their children in healthy ways. Thankfully, Pamela Bolen has used basic toys to reveal practical principles, as she guides the reader in how to develop character, reassurance, confidence and esteem in your children that will last for a life time.

— DEBBY WADE, MA, LMFT, LPC, CST

I just love this book! Pamela J. Bolen offers parents like me specific guidance on how to transform our kids into joyful, generous, and confident individuals ready to take on the world. Every chapter in *Parenting Out of the Box* ends with journaling questions I need to ponder about my parenting skills as well as fun family time activities to help my husband and I connect with our kids, promising love and laughter in our home for years to come!

— VICTORYA ROGERS, LIFE COACH/AUTHOR,
FINDING A MAN WORTH KEEPING

Pamela deals with a topic that I'm passionate about—teaching our children to be confident in how God made them, not just teaching them that they can do anything they want if they try hard enough. *Parenting Out of the Box* is a beautiful metaphor that helps us as parents, not only focus our children on their identity in Christ, but also helps us to understand how we can fulfill God's purpose for our lives!

— KAREN COVELL, FOUNDING DIRECTOR,
HOLLYWOOD PRAYER NETWORK

Every child needs a positive push and a boost of encouragement. Using the metaphor of a toy box, Pamela Bolen creatively opens our understanding of effective ways to build strength and courage into our kids' lives. As parents, we can always use fresh ideas. Pamela equips us with solid principles based on her own expertise as a counselor. Open up this book and dig in, you are sure to find parenting treasures!

— KAROL LADD, BESTSELLING AUTHOR
THE POWER OF A POSITIVE MOM

This book is dedicated to my family. Every day you have been in my life has been a blessing from God. Your creativity, humor and faith inspires me always.

PARENTING OUT OF THE BOX

*Secrets to Creating
Healthy Self-Esteem
in Kids and Teens*

Pamela J. Bolen, *LPC, LMFT*

TL

Thrilling Life Publishers
Southlake, Texas

Parenting Out of the Box
Secrets to Creating Healthy Self-Esteem in Kids and Teens
Published by
Thrilling Life Publishers
P.O. Box 92522
Southlake TX 76092
www.thrillinglife.com

Printed in the United States of America
International Standard Book Number: 978-0-9889240-0-0

Cover design by Micah Kandros Design
micahkandrosdesign.com

Cover photo by istock

Author Photo by Brock Christian Ramirez

Unless otherwise notated, Scripture quotations are taken
from the ESV® Bible, *Holy Bible, English Standard Version*®,
Copyright ©2001, by Crossway.

Names, gender, location and specifics of some of the stories
and anecdotes have been changed to protect the identities
of the persons involved.

Family/Parenting/Relationships
Thrilling Life Publishers
Helping you Pursue a Thrilling Life – John 10:10
www.thrillinglife.com
www.thrillinglife.com/parentingoutofthebox

Table of Contents

Acknowledgments

I WOULD FIRST OF ALL like to thank my mother, Joy Bolen for somehow putting up with all my antics as a child and for not turning me over to appropriate authorities. You taught me to laugh and find humor in the midst of life's stressors. You role modeled how to be a Christian, to always have faith in God, and to have confidence and self-esteem.

I have to thank my sister, Cindi Cary who provided much of the material in this book. Together we have shown others that if you are not caught for being a juvenile delinquent, you have the opportunity to still make something of yourself.

To my husband, Dr. Carlos Ramirez, thank you for all of your love and support during our marriage and in raising our 3 precious children. You are a wonderful husband and father. Thank you for not suing me for all the pranks I have done to you.

To my children, Colby you are always making me laugh with your creative wit. Lindzey, you are such an inspiration and have motivated me to finish this book. Thank you also for editing. Brock, you have been an incredible encourager. Thank you for your assistance in both computer technology and photography. My goal has always been for you three to have the self-esteem God destined you to have and to keep God first in your lives.

To my father-in-law and mother-in-law, Rudy and Elia Ramirez thank you for your love, support and generosity. It has been an adventure being in your family.

Jody Capehart, you have worked with me on this book for some time. Thank you for your editing ideas and creative suggestions. You have been wonderful. Chris Capehart, thank you for your input and your suggestions on revising text.

And last but you are never last in anything, Victorya Rogers my friend, editor, and publisher who encouraged me to write this book. Thank you. Despite my many efforts to give up, you never let me. You worked so many hours editing and evaluating. I could have never done this without you. From the first day that I met you when you said, "Why don't you write a book?" And then many, many days after that when you kept asking… Okay already!

Introduction

⁓

OUR LIVES BEGAN with toys. Whether soft cuddly bears or brightly colored mobiles, cooing baby dolls or magical musical sets, toys just seemed to be there waiting for our arrival. You may have even had a nursery filled with many toys, rattles, and stuffed animals before you released your first cry.

As wonderful as it is to give material gifts of precious toys to our children, no present, game, or toy comes close to the value of gifting them with an enduring positive self-concept, a gift that leads them towards becoming all God created them to be. The following pages reveal to parents some powerful secrets actually found hidden right inside your child's bedroom, in the toy box. That's right. The very toy box that has perhaps been there since the day you brought your child home from the hospital.

Treasure Hunt

It seems only fitting that such treasures from our beginning would play a vital role in our emotional development. Whether you are in a blended, traditional or single parent family, you will soon discover how the toys you've been tripping over hold a key to promoting healthy self-esteem in your children.

Toys bring so much joy, anticipation, laughter, fantasy, and even security to little ones around the world. Who didn't fall in love with the Pixar movie series *Toy Story* with Sheriff Woody and Buzz Lightyear? We all could relate to the fantasy of our beloved toys magically becoming alive. But developing positive self-esteem in your kids does not require a toy's transformation. So how do toys relate then to self-assurance? They offer parents insight into your current parenting skills so you can learn what works and what doesn't in helping you raise children who love themselves.

Parenting Out of the Box reveals metaphors for the common toys found in many children's toy boxes. Most likely your child's toy box contains variations of these cherished items that perfectly illustrate the development of lifelong, healthy self-esteem. Bet you never realized a few toys could hold the keys to shaping and influencing your child's future.

Every parent hopes for a positive self-image for their child or stepchild. Parents want kids to love themselves as much as they want their kids to know they are loved by the parents. But self-assurance and self-confidence doesn't just happen; it is taught.

Confident Security

Yes, it IS possible for children to grow up feeling confident and self-assured in an ever changing insecure world. Even in the midst of conflict and failure you can help your children develop a positive self-image. Kids don't have to be the most beautiful, most popular, or most successful to feel secure. Security comes from knowing you are loved and that you have value.

Many parents don't realize they play a prominent role in children learning to love or hate themselves. And some parents actually have no idea when they are behaving in such a way as to harm their child's self-worth.

But there is a difference between healthy self-esteem and entitlement. Sadly, we are in an age of entitlement when too many children are growing up with little to no concept of responsibility and refusing to move out upon adulthood. Too many are feeling entitled to have Mom and Dad provide for them financially into the 30s, 40s and beyond, while their parents wonder how in the world did they get there!

The kids today, who feel entitled, do so because their parents didn't train them up to have a healthy self-esteem. They didn't learn to do things on their own. They didn't learn consequences for their choices. Rather, they learned that when life gets tough and unpleasant, Mom and Dad step in to fix it and rescue.

Yet, our society is learning that over-indulging and rescuing children from every stress or crisis doesn't develop healthy self-image, but rather it develops unending dependence and entitlement.

God Made You for a Purpose

Having healthy self-esteem is not about unrealistically pumping your child up to be King of the World. It seems that some people are overly concerned that self-esteem is simply self-indulgence. Quite the opposite is true. Healthy self-esteem is accepting that God made you for a purpose. People often assume when you talk about child self-esteem that parents are trying to convince their children that they can do anything they want. This book is not about that because it is just not true. In *Unleash!*, Author and Pastor Perry Noble talks about this being "The Great American Lie."

> I am about six feet six inches tall, and I weigh around 225 pounds. With that information in mind, what if I told you I really wanted to be a jockey and it was my dream to ride the winning horse in the Kentucky Derby? Be honest—you'd probably laugh a little and say, 'Dude, at your size, the horse might actually try to ride you.' I am not the size, shape, or weight needed to be a successful jockey. No matter how much I believed in myself and no matter how hard I tried, I would only wind up feeling like a failure. I'd be a fool to

dedicate my life to something I was obviously not created to do.[1]

Good intentioned and well-meaning parents unknowingly make mistakes. I hope you find answers on these pages and change things that need correcting. With God, nothing is impossible—the longer you wait to change things the quicker the years pass and the harder it will be to create change. But you picked up this book today, which reveals you are intrigued with the idea of raising healthy kids and you are willing to make change where necessary. You can do this.

Growing Independent Future Adults

I understand you. We all love our kids and we want to do everything for them. We want to give them everything we didn't have. But we can't do that if we want them to grow to be independent and become who they were born to be.

This book is your journey into becoming the parent you were born to be as you help your child become the child he was born to be. To become that parent takes an inside look. It takes a willingness to see what you are doing wrong as well as acknowledging what you are already doing right.

As you see each of the secrets I reveal through each toy we explore, you will see some things you are doing well already and some things, well not so much. But that is ok. Life is about the journey. We make mistakes. It's about admitting them, making amends and turning the opposite direction.

Congratulations for picking up this book. You care about raising self-assured, confident, independent children with a healthy self-esteem.

Inspiring Better Choices

That's why I wrote this book: to help parents look inside their parenting skills and see where they can modify and fine tune when needed. My hope is that you will be inspired to stop behaviors that have unknowingly been crushing your child's spirit and adapt behaviors and creative ideas that will build lifelong, healthy self-esteem, for both you and your children.

How did I come to write a book about toys teaching parenting skills? As my own children outgrew their toy box and beloved memories flooded my mind as I collected them for storage in the attic, it hit me how each of them easily represented the lessons and skills I have been teaching my clients for decades.

So Tired of Seeing the Struggle

I had to write this book because I'm so tired of seeing people struggle because of how they feel about themselves. Over three decades of seeing children, teens, and adults held back emotionally motivated me to share the same secrets I've shared with clients. I have seen kids progress academically and socially because of gaining confidence. I've been honored to witness adults improve in their marriage, family and work place because they quit believing lies about themselves and replaced it with feelings of value.

I have seen clients of all ages totally turn their world around because they simply started becoming more optimistic. They gained assurance and quit believing they were "losers who wouldn't amount to anything." They learned to quit buying into the unhealthy, negative criticisms from the past and broke free to embrace the opportunity to excel. You and your children can do the same.

Feeling like you are worth something can change your course and destination. You no longer have to allow the past to dictate the future. Gaining a healthy self-image can be life altering for those without one. And you can't teach your children to have a healthy self-esteem if you don't possess one yourself.

Feel Good About Yourself

Each of these skills show parents how to teach their children to recognize their own value and worth as the parent accepts his or her own. And seeing one's value leads to a healthy self-concept that indicates you like yourself and you appreciate how God made you, even with all your imperfections!

Wouldn't you like to feel great about yourself? Better yet, would you like for your kids to experience the joy, peace, and security of positive self-esteem, beginning at an early age and continuing through a lifetime? The gift of self-esteem and the gift of confidence are two of the most important blessings you can instill in your child. Let's dive into your child's toy box and find all the tools you need to be all that.

In the pages that follow we will examine beloved toys to reveal what role they can play in your child's development. These 10 toys depicted are actually metaphors for how to build healthy self-esteem in your child, teen, or self. Those toys are the Compass, emergency rescue vehicles, the board games of Battleship® and Sorry®, mirror, Silly String®, bubbles, Pom Poms, train, and medical kit.

Allow the metaphor of the toy box to teach you the parenting secrets to developing lifelong, healthy self-esteem in each and every one of your kids. My goal is to open the eyes of loving parents so you can see how every word you say and every action you take affects your children for better or worse for the rest of their lives.

Box Talks

Each chapter ends with a "Box Talks" section for you to interact with the material. First, there are journaling questions for you to ponder and react to the chapter—how did the toy discussed challenge you? Have your journal ready to write out your "Aha" moments. The second part of Box Talks is for you to interact with your family. All the Box Talks were written with fun family time in mind.

CHAPTER 1

The Compass

"Families are the compass that guide us. They
are the inspiration to reach great heights and
our comfort when we occasionally falter."

— ALAIN CORRE

WAS WORKING WITH A FAMILY that had a teenage
daughter who had become quite the challenge. She
would not come home at the agreed upon time. She
was drinking alcohol, smoking pot, having sex and
rarely attending high school. Her irresponsibility also
included mounting speeding tickets. That is when
they called for an appointment with me. At our first
appointment I asked the father if he thought part of
the problem was the friends she was choosing. To

this he responded, "No, her friends aren't the bad influence. She is."

This was the very first time I had heard a parent put the responsibility directly on his child, rather than blaming everyone else. It was actually very refreshing. I knew right then there was hope for this family.

Yes, anyone's behavior is inevitably influenced by whom he spends the most of his time. But, when it comes to friends, choosing to be around a person is ultimately up to the individual. His daughter has a will to choose, and she was using that will to hang with the wrong crowd and in doing so, choosing to engage in those activities by her own free will.

Within a short period of time, thankfully, that family was able to turn things around in a positive direction, and the daughter worked on her issues successfully.

❖   ❖   ❖

The Compass
The compass, that little circular device with the N, S, E & W written on it with a needle changing every move you make. Which way shall we go? Which way shall we turn? What does it all mean? You probably have one from a survival or camping kit that your child received as a toy. It probably doesn't work very well because it has been discarded to the bottom of the box. Things, however, don't always have to operate as we think they should to still deliver a benefit.

The Compass

In Isaiah 42:16 it says, "And I will lead the blind in a way that they do not know, in paths that they have not known I will guide them." We desperately need God as our compass. He is ready, willing and able to guide you through every turn of life, and that includes parenting. We are lost and forever searching until we accept that truth.

The compass serves as a reminder to us that every circumstance can be viewed from different directions. In navigation, altering your course just a few degrees will completely change your destination—same with parenting. A fresh approach to parenting may be all you need to begin seeing vast improvement in your child's self-esteem. There are many creative ways to gain that fresh approach to build your child's self-worth. You just need a little inspiration.

Driving in a Different Direction

On my 16th birthday I was given my first car. My 15-year-old sister was not given a car because it wasn't her birthday and she didn't have a driver's license. She apparently had a problem with this as several days a week I would notice that my car was mysteriously out of gasoline. This was extremely frustrating as I was clearly not driving often enough to drain my gas tank every few days. In fact, I wasn't driving often enough to empty a tank in a week!

I knew somehow my sister was sneaking my car out when I was either away from the house or asleep in my room. So I began clocking the mileage to set a trap. Yet, every day the mileage was the same I had written. She didn't seem to be driving my car, but I also did not have a leak in my tank. I knew she was doing something, but I could never understand or prove what!

It was many decades later that she finally confessed to what had happened to my vanishing gasoline. My sister had indeed used my car for an entire year and a half without ever getting caught. How did she do it? She drove my car *backwards*. Yes, she drove it in reverse! You see, the odometer will not advance if you are not going forward. My sister figured that out quickly. So she drove my car all over town in the middle of the night and was never caught. You would think she sort of stood out as a driver going in reverse, but the police never caught her. And sadly, neither did she get caught by my unsuspecting mother and worst of all, me!

In *Praying for Your Prodigal Daughter,* author Janet Thompson writes, "When we start out on a cross-country trip, we know we're not going to arrive in a day. Every town gets us closer to our destination, but they aren't our final goal. Yet without covering that ground, we'd never complete the trip and reach our journey's end."[2]

Sometimes you can arrive to the place you want to be, but in ways you never thought possible. You may be able to positively impact your child's self-esteem just by taking a different path, even when it feels like you're driving backwards. You possess the creativity to enhance and improve how your child views himself and feels about himself. You just may not realize it yet.

Verbalize Praise

What words of encouragement or praise could you share with your child today that would light up their face and heart? What traits do you admire in your child or stepchild that you have identified but have not verbalized? They need to hear it! Many times when I meet family members of my counseling clients, I relay that I've heard so many nice things about them. Most people are very surprised. The usual response is "Really?"

It seems that we all think more positively about our loved ones than we actually verbalize to them. You have an opportunity today to change that! Take a few moments right now to tell your children individually about their positive characteristics. Let them know what you appreciate, what you are grateful for, and how much you love them for who they are. They may think that you've started happy hour a little early, but soon it will become a habit, and sharing positive compliments will be a normal occurrence in your family.

During the many years of my counseling practice, my primary objective has been to teach clients how to problem solve. If a client is dependent on me to solve all of their issues, that may build my job security but it doesn't promote my client's emotional security. Many years ago my oldest son asked me about my job as a therapist. He was curious about how it all worked.

"So Mom," he asked, "Do people actually come in and have you tell them exactly what to do about every problem they have?"

I thoughtfully replied, "Well actually, I teach people how to problem solve so they can talk about it then make their own decisions on what to do."

He looked very confused.

"You mean people come in and pay you all that money, and you don't even tell them what to do? Mom, I don't want to hurt your feelings, but I don't think anyone is going to come back to you for just that!"

I had to laugh, because the truth is I didn't get into counseling for job security. I got into counseling to help families find emotional security. And one way to work towards emotional security is to tap into your creative side to get your creative juices flowing. You have it in you to problem solve. Let the compass remind you that you have the option to choose what direction to go in your parenting and that will indeed take a lot of creativity! But the good news is that every single person has creativity inside them because you were made by a creative God! Thus, having not yet tapped into your creative side in no way negates that you have a creative side!

Think about your own individual child. What motivates your child to be a better person? What encouraging words could you say to your child that would steer him toward making better choices? Usually, the more you praise someone for a certain characteristic, the more often you will see that characteristic repeated.

Reward Positive Behavior

Remember behavior modification from Psychology 101? Basically, by rewarding positive behavior (rewards can be verbal praise), you can motivate the individual to repeat the desired behavior. For example, if you make a big deal when your child gives away one of their favorite possessions and then you compliment how giving, unselfish, and kind she is, then you have planted huge seeds in her heart. Those seeds will spring a garden to flourish for a lifetime. Your child will not only feel good about giving, but she will also want to continue giving because it will make her feel good about herself.

One of the qualities people with healthy self-esteem possess is that they are kind and giving to others. Personally, when I reach out to someone in need, I never know whether I am doing it because it makes me feel happy or because it makes the person feel happy. Perhaps it is both. It just feels wonderful to bless someone else.

If you want to develop lifelong self-esteem, teach your child to give generously of themselves. How do you teach a child generosity? By being generous yourself, they will imitate you. It always shifts back to that. What you role model is what they learn, conscious or unconscious. If you want your child to become generous, he needs to see you being generous on a regular basis. The same goes for whatever traits you want to instill.

You are under constant, recorded surveillance, which will be replayed over and over. Kids may not remember to take their homework to school, but they remember every time we say one thing but live another. Sorry about the pressure, but it is undeniable. Take an inside look at your behavior around your children. And if you see you are not getting the results you want, perhaps it is time to try a different direction. By the way, you won't be perfect. None of us are.

Please do not read this and feel guilty about your shortcomings as a parent. We all have them. Here's a story that will make you feel better. Many years ago a client came in for her session and said she had had a very good week. When I asked what made it so good, she replied it was because of me. Feeling rather proud, I asked what I had done.

"I saw you getting all your kids in the car at the baseball park on Saturday. It made my week to see that you were normal like the rest of us."

Tired of Being Normal

It made me feel horrible because "normal" probably meant I was yelling and screaming at my kids to hurry and get in the car and put their seat belts on! That session changed my life. I didn't want to be "normal" anymore. From that point on, I tried to treat my family as if all my clients were watching at all times. I'm not perfect and still make mistakes, even though I try. So please don't feel guilty if you see yourself in many of the examples I write in this book. Take it as a wake up call to change directions by moving just a few degrees to the right or left of your compass. Starting today is better than starting next year or never starting at all.

Strive to be on your best behavior for the sake of the next generation. Strive to be consistent in word and deed. Strive to be an encouraging, uplifting, positive parent. What you do, they learn, even more than what you say.

My mother had my sister and me in church literally every time the doors were open. We went to Sunday school, then "big" Church, and then Church again on Sunday night. We attended Wednesday night service and were also in a mid-week Bible study. In the 8th grade I decided that I had gone to church as much as I needed. I felt that I was good. I was right up there with the angels and probably had some church credit for attending so often.

So the Sunday morning came when I decided to break the news to my mom that I wasn't going to church that day.

She was not happy.

I don't know how she got me to still go to church that day, but as we were sitting together in the pew I turned and announced, "I'm not wearing any clothes under this raincoat."

She apparently did not believe me and said, "You most certainly are!"

So I opened the left side of my red raincoat and whispered, "You can make me go to church, but you can't make me wear clothes!"

I guess you now see I had a bit of defiance in me. Now you understand why I was in church so often! If there was hope for me, there is certainly hope for you!

People tell me they don't go to church because they were forced to as a child. They say they do not want to do that to their children. Your job as a parent is to guide your kids towards healthy habits—even when they don't want to learn them.

Teaching Essential Skills

We force our kids to brush their teeth. We force them to go to school and do their homework. We force them to change out of dirty, nasty clothes. There are essential life habits and skills parents or someone must instill in children, even when met with resistance. It's hard to find anyone these days who doesn't feel they could use therapy for *something* their parent did or didn't do. It might as well be for encouraging your kids to attend a positive church. Even if you are met with similar resistance as I gave to my mother, it is worth the effort to provide moral and spiritual training to your child.

My mom didn't scare me into going to church. She just somehow coerced and motivated me to actually want to go most of the time. Pastor Matt Chandler says, "Heaven is not a place for those who are afraid of hell; it's a place for those who love God. You can scare people into coming to your church, you can scare people into trying to be good, you can scare people into giving money, you can even scare them into walking down an aisle and praying a certain prayer, but you cannot scare people into loving God. You can't do it."[3] My mom showed me how to love God. She did that by taking me to church and by living out her faith the rest of the week.

No church is perfect because people go there and people aren't perfect.

Here are some tips on how to find a home church:

- *Make sure the pastor teaches the Bible and the messages line up with God's word.*
- *Make sure there is a children's/youth program that they enjoy.*
- *Make sure it is a church that reaches out to others in need.*
- *Make sure it is a church where you are encouraged, challenged and are spiritually growing.*

Using Your Compass

Perhaps you need the compass to move in a different direction. Charting new territory can be an adventure. It can be interesting to travel where you have not gone before. Yes, if you are going to positively affect your child's self-confidence, you will need all the creative direction possible. Get ideas from your friends or children's teachers. I learn from my clients every day. There has rarely been a day I haven't been blessed with a story from a coworker or client. I get new material everyday of what to do or more so what not to do.

Just like a car's GPS recalculates whenever you mess up and make a wrong turn, you can always get back on track when you turn to God for help. Even if it feels like you are driving in reverse, you may still get to your final destination. It worked for at least one 15 year old sister that I know.

Box Talks

Journal Time

1. Did the compass spark any Aha moments for you? If so, where do need to navigate a few degrees right or left?

2. We talked about finding our creative side. List 4 creative things you have done.

3. Have you found you forget to compliment your kids on their small accomplishments? Write out 5 things you can compliment each of your kids for this week and then do so.

4. When you read about your kids learning through imitating your behavior—good or bad—what came to mind? What have you seen your kids do that you realize they got from you?

Family Time

1. Plan to have a least one local family outing every month (once a week would be wonderful). Get everyone involved in planning the get-togethers. Perhaps let each family member take turns in choosing where you go. Here are some ideas: movies, zoo, museum, park, mall, restaurant, biking, hiking, paintball, go carts, miniature golf, amusement park or picnic.

2. Make it an evening event for your family to sit down and plan some destinations for the next family trip. Have each member research where he would like to go and present it to the family along with activities to do during the trip. Even young children can participate in this family planning adventure.

CHAPTER 2

The Emergency Rescue Vehicles

"Whether your child is 3 or 13, don't rush
in to rescue him until you know he's
done all he can to rescue himself."

— Barbara F. Meltz

A VERY SWEET COUPLE came in for counseling. Their
son was struggling. The parents wanted him to
get a job. The son didn't want to get a job. The parents
wanted him to finish school. The son didn't want to
finish school. The parents wanted him to move out.
The son had no desire to move out.

That son was 38. He had been coddled, enabled,
rescued, and spoiled for 37 years. His parents never

forced him to move out. They feared it would be mean and uncaring even though it was a hardship on them to support him over the decades. He on the other hand was enjoying his entitlement and considered it a major step down to move out. He has never supported himself and has no plans to begin. He had been raised to be a master manipulator of his parents, with guilt as his favorite weapon.

His frustration? He just cannot understand why he can't get a date. My advice to him was for the parents to rent the Matthew McConaughey film "Failure to Launch," and watch it with their son because it reflected their life together.

❖   ❖   ❖

Emergency Rescue Vehicles

Emergency Rescue Vehicles are found in every toy box. Most of those trucks are pretty banged up due to frequent use. This mode of toy transportation is a must for any child's play and sense of adventure. You'll find them equipped with lights, horns, ladders, tools and gadgets. These rescue machines are ready to save the day anywhere, anytime an emergency pops in the mind of children in Toyville.

Does that sound like your parenting style in the real world? Every time your child needs rescuing from *anything*, YOU ARE THERE, 24 hours a day without notice or without reservations. It does not matter what you have planned for the day. You've taught your child you are not important. Your life takes a distant 2nd to The Cause. The priority for the moment is to rescue at all cost and at any expense. You drop every plan and commitment for the day to board the Emergency Rescue Vehicle because you are needed. You are committed to the rescue.

If you keep this up, you'll eventually need to be committed to a psychiatric ward as it becomes increasingly difficult to constantly pull off rescues with little to no notice. It may look something like this.

Phone rings!

Dad: "Hello."

Daughter: "Dad, hey I'm really sorry but I forgot my math homework again. Could you drop all your plans, bring it immediately, reschedule your meeting with the President of the United States and leave for school right now?"

Dad: "I thought you were working on being more responsible. I cannot get away from work right now. Besides I canceled with the President last week to bring you your Science project!"

Daughter: "Please Dad please! I'm begging you. It's the last time. I promise! This is very important. I've got to have your help!"

Dad: "I told you last time that I was not going to rescue you any more. You have to learn responsibility. Last time was the last time. I'm sorry."

Daughter: (Last effort, using guilt, manipulation, tears, and anything that will close the deal) "You're not sorry! If you were you would WANT to help me. Please Dad one last time. Dad, I can't believe you want me to fail! If I don't turn this math in today my life is over! Everybody makes mistakes. I bet you have forgotten something in your lifetime. What have I ever done to you that would make you do this to me? (Now beginning to sob) Dad I don't know what I'll do! Please I promise this really is the last time I'll ever ask a favor of you for the rest of my life. Please!"

Dad: (heavy sigh) "Alright. I'll be right there."

How many times do parents give in and do exactly what they know in their gut is unwise in teaching responsibility? More importantly, why? Parents give in and rescue because it is distressing to see children fail. It is difficult to say, "No," when a negative consequence will follow.

In this example Dad gave in and rescued because he didn't want his child to get a bad grade. Let's follow through this thought process. A bad parent would refuse to take the math homework to school, right? Then that bad parent's child would probably fail math. Since the poor child failed math, he would lose confidence in himself for other classes. He would then fail all other subjects and be held back from the next grade. His GPA would fall so low that he would never get into college. He'd then be forced to take the only employment available to someone with such a bad parent—a park bench gum scraper. And he became that park bench gum scraper all because his Dad would not take math homework to him in elementary school.

Don't Send Out the Rescue Vehicle Just Because the Phone Rings

It is just about as ridiculous as that. When you send out the Emergency Rescue Vehicles unnecessarily, you do so out of fear that your child can't survive without your intervention. Reality is he desperately needs to be trained to eventually do exactly that—survive without your intervention. When you constantly rush to the rescue, you are damaging your child's self-confidence and rewarding his irresponsibility. In essence you are conveying to the child that the way he is handling his life is acceptable with no consequences for his irresponsibility. Sure, he may have to endure a few lectures from you, but that's a small price to pay for getting "off the hook" once again.

Will Rogers put it well when he said, "If you find yourself in a hole, the first thing to do is stop digging." If your child is digging his own hole, don't provide him with a bigger shovel. Rescuing him just ensures that the next hole will be bigger and deeper.

Have children at any age do as much for their selves as possible. It builds confidence. It builds a feeling of self-assurance. It builds their self-esteem. When you do everything for your kids, it may make them feel good about you, but it won't build confidence in their own abilities.

If your child takes five minutes to button his own shirt, and it takes you seven seconds to do it for him, set your alarm for five minutes earlier and let him button it. He needs to learn. The development of self-esteem is worth far more than five more minutes of sleep.

If you are a perfectionist or your Obsessive Compulsive Disorder is acting up, then you will have difficulty with this next suggestion. I certainly relate. If your child is making his bed, don't go back in there and make it perfectly. Your home is not on The Christmas Tour this year. The bed is fine. You should be thrilled your kid can and will make a bed. When you go and redo their chores, they begin to feel like they can't do anything right. It is extremely frustrating to children to feel as though they never measure up.

Parents have such a tendency to take over and try to do it all. That is not what is best for the child. At some point, children, teenagers, and adults have to take care of their own business. Parents tend to take over what should be the responsibility of the child. Unfortunately, it may be more about parents "looking good" to other adults than the child actually learning the lesson necessary for becoming a successful adult. Subconsciously, parents may be unaware they are actually sabotaging the development of their child. But they are.

A parent may fear that a child not turning in his math homework may suggest that the uninvolved, irresponsible parents were watching a Lifetime movie the evening prior, rather than compiling homework in the neglected child's backpack. Too often parents are preoccupied with how *they* appear to others. Let your child get a poor grade on a homework paper in 5th grade rather than eventually failing 10th grade. At some point, you cannot rescue anymore. It becomes all too time consuming and physically impossible.

Carrying Life Preservers

What is really worse is that you end up resenting your child's behavior. Yet you have worked so diligently to reinforce the very behavior you now cannot stand. It can make a person insane. I personally know a little about rescuing. I carry life preservers in my car.

Care enough about your child to make them accountable. You are not helping by rescuing. Rather it is very hurtful and damaging. Enabling negative behaviors reinforce continued irresponsible decisions. Delaying the inevitable by continuing the rescue creates larger and more difficult problems down the road. Stop the rescue when he is a child, or you will end up trying to get your 40-year-old son to move out and into his own place.

A child who does not learn responsibility in basic areas may be crippled for life. If you happen to be married to such an individual, you know the frustration and exasperation I am referring to here.

Stop being part of the problem in your child's future by allowing this to continue. He or she may not thank you now but their future spouse will thank you later. It comes down to setting boundaries. And some of the best information on boundary setting is found in the boundaries book series by Drs. Cloud and Townsend. *Boundaries with Kids* is an excellent guide relevant for any parent. In their chapter "Kids Need Parents With Boundaries," they state "'If you can't stand the heat, stay out of the kitchen' goes the old saying. Part of the heat of parenting is tolerating and enduring your child's hatred of your boundaries. You and your child each have a different job here: The kid's job is to test your resolve, so she can learn about reality. Your job is to withstand the test, including anger, pouting, tantrums, and much more."[4] I know this is excruciatingly hard for parents who just want their kids to be happy and pain free. Hear me on this, you are not a being a cold, heartless parent by setting boundaries. Having guidelines for expected behavior is part of being a responsible adult. It is what makes your kids feel secure. Set boundaries and stick to them even when it hurts you, and it will! It is very difficult to see your child experience the negative consequences of their behavior.

It Can Hurt to be a Good Parent

When my own children were young, there would be times after they received consequences for their actions that I would go into my room and cry privately because they missed out on something important to them. Kids believe parents relish in the glorious moments of their sentencing. They are convinced we wouldn't issue negative consequences if we didn't like doing it, especially when we have the power to make the punishment go away. I suppose I understand a little how God feels when faced with the same situation.

Although I'm focusing on teaching your children to be more responsible and less dependent, there is a small portion of children who will not be able to accomplish this as easily. He or she may have emotional or neurological problems that prohibit their ability. If you suspect that your child has Attention Deficit Hyperactivity Disorder (ADHD) or other focusing issues, you may need to pursue additional professional help. Children with these types of challenges may be unable to change certain behaviors on their own. Don't allow this to be an excuse for you to continue rescuing, however. It is imperative that you seek professional consultation so that your child will experience a successful life. There are some wonderful studies and available books from experts on the topic to help you gain further insight on how to work with these challenges. With love, focus and proper training, even kids with challenges like ADHD can learn to live a rewarding life of self-sufficiency.

Loving More Than I Was Loved

I can remember very well being grounded as a teenager. And that was just for the things I got caught for. I would be sitting home bored, mad, disenchanted with life, telling God that when I was a parent I would never punish my children. I would love them more than I was loved. I would never purposely force them to be miserable just to be taught "some lesson."

The parents who fail to teach that life has consequences are not effectively preparing kids for life outside the home. As you mature, you realize some of the hardest moments in life are the ones you hoped you'd never see. If you don't turn in any homework, you will fail. If you keep showing up late for work, you will get fired. If you post careless pictures on the Internet, you could lose your scholarship or your job. If you steal, you could end up in jail. These are just a few examples of real life painful consequences that will be handed out by other authority figures when the lessons are not taught in the home.

If you cannot or have not followed through with punishment, consider getting professional help to determine what is happening or has happened that makes it so impossible for you to follow through. Proverbs 12:1 states, "Whoever loves discipline loves knowledge, but he who hates reproof is stupid." Hebrews 12:11 says, "For the moment all discipline seems painful rather than pleasant, but later it yields the peaceful fruit of righteousness to those who have been trained by it."

I've often been asked what would be effective discipline. This again, takes creativity to determine what will be most effective with your child's personality. Appropriate discipline might include restriction of electronic devices like their cell phone, computer or play systems. You might also consider restriction of social activities. These types of consequences are quite motivating to convince behavioral change. If these don't work then get more creative. Some parents have taken their child's door off their bedroom until change occurred. Determine what would be the most motivating for your child. My kids have had to pay $20.00 for disobeying. It worked. It turns out parting with $20.00 is extremely motivating to a teenager.

Training children to reach their full potential is an awesome responsibility. Too often parents rescue their children from poor decisions, thus they don't learn from their mistakes. If you bail your child out every time they do something wrong, you are teaching and training him to be reckless and negligent. It is not a good sign if you have the bail bondsman's phone number memorized.

Shifting From Entitlement

Teach a child to live within their means. This has become a growing epidemic as parents tend to overspend and indulge their offspring because they have the ability to do so. This generation of children, teenagers, and college-aged adults have a strong sense of entitlement. They have been blessed financially by their parents but feel they are *owed* it rather than being grateful for it.

If your child expects material possessions that are over and above your duty to them, reevaluate your position. I have literally seen a family in counseling because the daughter is upset and depressed that her parents won't buy her $1700 Jimmy Choo shoes. This is when I am thankful that before I majored in Psychology, I was a Drama major. I use acting techniques more on a daily basis than I ever use psychology. Keeping a professional demeanor and facial response when a family is arguing over $1700 shoes deserves, in the very least, an Academy Award nomination.

Kids Need to Earn Their Own Success

Don't be offended or feel guilty if you can relate to this, just consider beginning to make different decisions. You may be able to afford expensive shoes, but a young person starting out their independent life probably cannot. Children and teenagers believe they should live the same lifestyle when they move out as they do at home with their parents. More than likely it took years of education and/or years of working long hours to attain what you have today. Too many teens and young adults don't want to invest the time it takes to earn successful life. They expect Mommy and Daddy to do all the work, while they lazily continue to enjoy the benefits. Don't let this be your family.

Teaching a child to live within their means could be illustrated by giving your child $15.00 a week for lunch money. If a teen unwisely spends it for other purchases or overspends for several days, do you feel sorry for him and give him extra cash? No, he gets to take a peanut butter sandwich that he makes himself.

"But he really doesn't like peanut butter," you tell me. "Don't you feel badly that he ran out of money? He is just a kid. Certainly you made mistakes when you were a kid too and still do. Besides he will probably go without eating if not given the money, which is even worse. So what is the harm in slipping him a few extra dollars?"

It is not just a few dollars, and it will be your child's choice if chooses not to eat the sandwich. The harm is in how you are training him to deal with life—run to Mom and Dad, and everything will be fixed. You will find yourself repeating that pattern in every area of his life, constantly rewarding any irresponsible choice. It is inevitable that much larger, poorer decisions in his life will follow because he hasn't learned.

You either learn it in the small things so you can master the big things or you just don't ever learn it. This little event of spending all the lunch money early can become the foundation and script for how your family handles all future issues.

Stop the Rescue

If you cannot stop yourself from rescuing at this very elementary level, then you are going to have great difficulty when serious problems surface. Stop feeling guilty and stop rescuing. Breathe deeply, release the guilt (it isn't even warranted) and free yourself from feeling like you are being mean; You will be making a meaningful decision to steer your child in a positive, responsible direction. You are showing more love than ever. It probably is not going to be comfortable for you or your child. Parenting rarely is. But I promise it will pay off.

Remember when your children were little and they wanted to eat candy for dinner? Did you feel badly for redirecting them and feeding them solid nutritious food? Hopefully you didn't. That is what you are going to be doing now. You are choosing to deal with your child in a way that is best for her. It may not make you feel good at the moment but the long-term effects are tremendous.

If you don't get a handle on this behavior with your child now, you will want to be trading in your little darlings later when they drive you crazy from the pattern you established. Your child knows all too well if you are going to mop up, clean up, and fix up their mess or not. Once kids realize that the manipulating, scamming, scheming, and lying won't be tolerated; things gradually get more normal. 3 John 4 says, "I have no greater joy than to hear that my children are walking in the truth." Change things up as of today and trade in your janitor uniform because every time you rescue, mop, clean, and fix their chaos, you make it more difficult for the next time.

You didn't really believe this would be the last time, did you? When you send out the Emergency Rescue Vehicle without an emergency, you are cementing unhealthy responses to common issues. An airplane is flying in the sky with a banner boldly displaying, "I will always take care of your problems so you never have to." How well does a person feel about himself when his parents have to save him from intermittent disasters? It is humiliating, embarrassing, depressing and extremely self-esteem deflating.

"But," you may be thinking, "If I don't save her, she may drown." She is not going to drown. She may, however have to get a little water up her nose. Often lessons are not learned until one gets a little wet.

Equip Your Teen for Independence

The latest statistics indicate that 100% of us will die. You will not always be there for your children. Sure, you hope to be around until they grow up and maybe until their grandbabies have babies. But you just don't know. Equip your children to be able to exist and succeed apart from you. Self-sufficiency builds self-esteem and confidence. What greater reward than for a parent to have children who grow up able to take care of themselves and their own families! Sadly that is not the norm these days, but it should be.

I have often told clients that God is capable of anything and everything. He can do miracles. He can do anything. He could even make my breakfast every morning. Up to this moment, however, he has not chosen to deliver my breakfast. Apparently, God wants me to be able to feed myself. Perhaps it helps me to be more responsible, less lazy and less self-centered. Or maybe it has something to do with that group of Israelites wandering in the desert all those years. He did make their breakfast, and all they did was complain. "And the people spoke against God and against Moses, "Why have you brought us up out of Egypt to die in the wilderness? For there is no food and no water, and we loathe this worthless food." Numbers 21:5

There's an old Chinese proverb that says, "Give a man a fish, and you feed him for a day. Teach a man to fish, and you feed him for a lifetime." Teach your children to make their own breakfast. Teach them to do chores. Teach them to budget. Teach them to survive. Teach them to know God. Care more about your child's long-term welfare than your own comfort zone. Parenting can be emotionally painful. It can hurt and make you feel like a terrible parent to say, "No," to your child. If she doesn't hear it now from you, then she will hear it later from somebody else. Let her gain experience under your supervision. Your on the job training program will equip her for future success.

Rescuing is Exhausting

Many parents are not saying, "No," enough. Your teen or young adult will eventually get his first job. If he hasn't had to deal with the reality of "No" before, he definitely will have to then. Your child has to learn accountability and responsibility. There is a learning process that takes time. It can start as a preschooler or never develop. It is totally up to the parents. What a difficult and hard life it will be for someone who has always been rescued and never taught responsibility. If you insist on continuing to rescue, perhaps I should recommend you schedule a series of B-12 shots. The physical and emotional energy it takes to pull off these rescues is exorbitant. No one wins. No one feels good about the rescues, and the cost is more than anyone can afford. You are delaying what you eventually will be forced to confront.

There was a terrible flood in the spring. It had rained so much that flood waters reached to the tops of many roofs. It was truly horrifying. One man had managed to escape the waters and was stranded in a tree, desperately holding on for dear life. Terrified, he prayed like he had never prayed before for his rescue.

"Oh dear God, I am scared to death. I've seen people swept away in the raging waters. Please God, please save me! Please rescue me from this horrible flood. I beg you. I don't want to die like this," he pleaded.

Soon a helicopter flew by, let down a rope ladder and welcomed the man aboard.

"No, go away! The Lord will save me!" the man told the pilot.

Next, as the water rose higher and higher, a motorized boat offered assistance, but the man turned it away as well.

"I don't need saving! The Lord is going to rescue me!"

Later another helicopter hovered overhead while the pilot screamed out for the stranded man to grab the rope he had released. The pilot begged him to get onboard. Again he refused, stating that God was going to rescue him. The rain continued to pour, the water kept rising, and sadly, the man drowned.

As he entered the gates of heaven and met Saint Peter, the confused and upset man implored "Saint Peter, I have been a faithful and good man for all my life. Why didn't God rescue me?"

Saint Peter replied, "For goodness sake! He sent you two helicopters and a boat! What more do you want?"

The way you choose to help your children may not be their idea of the best rescue. It may feel like he is begging you for another rescue. You may send counseling. You may send rehabilitation. You may send a friend who's had the same problem.

Those are the same as the two helicopters and the boat. Those are appropriate and healthy ways to aid. Rescuing without instruction will only result in continual rescuing. Sometimes you need to evacuate when it begins to sprinkle.

Noah began building the ark and up to that point had probably never seen rain. Being prepared is a skill that is taught. Part of learning responsibility is recognizing how to be prepared for adversity. If you always swoop in and save the day before adversity hits, then your child never learns coping skills to deal with life.

An individual with healthy self-esteem has the ability to deal with problems and stress without relying on others. That person becomes independent, self-reliant and successful. As parents, we need to be constantly working ourselves out of a job. Your child will always need you. It is nicer however, for her to need you to meet her for lunch rather than to need you to bail her out of jail.

Don't be Resistant to Being Consistent

One of the biggest problems I encounter in my office is parents struggling with consistency. If you issue a rule, boundary, or consequence no matter what, keep your word. Teach your children that you are a person of your word. Help them to understand that if you say something then it is going to happen; there is a 100% chance that it will. If you tell your daughter that if she sneaks out of the house again, she will miss her Senior Prom and then she sneaks out anyway, she has got to miss her Senior Prom. She made the choice to break the rule, so she chose to miss it. It was totally within her ability to prevent the consequence from happening.

Be careful what you threaten because kids, especially teens, know if you will end up feeling sorry and negate the punishment. It is absolutely imperative that if you threaten a potential consequence then you enforce it, otherwise it means nothing. You better make believers out of your offspring, or you have no authority over them. Children will see you as all talk and no action. You will be left with no credibility when you desperately need it.

It is actually better to have no consequence for a poor choice than to proclaim one and then recant it. Children and teenagers in my office tell me for the most part that they have a 50% chance of getting off of a punishment early or never having the punishment at all. With those kinds of odds it is worth the gamble to most kids. Many teens brag to me about how they can manipulate their parents with guilt and get their way.

If you choose to become dedicated to being consistent it shouldn't take long to correct whatever challenges you are facing now. This may include having to leave an expensive amusement park shortly after arriving. If you've made it clear to your kids that unacceptable behavior will result in leaving the park, then you must follow through. If your kids think you are bluffing, they won't for long. You will only have to do this once and generally it is less expensive than therapy.

Be a Person of your Word

Follow through with consequences so the children in your home will believe every single word you say. Be consistent. It builds self-esteem in your child. Being a person of your word builds security for them because they now know if you say it, you mean it. Wavering and being unpredictable is what perpetuates the need to rescue. You will not always be available. At some point your child needs to be responsible. So why not now? Retire the Emergency Rescue Vehicle and save it for its real purpose, an emergency!

The Fire Truck

Another type of Emergency Rescue Vehicle that is necessary for a rescue is the Fire Truck. Now here is a toy in the box that really is for emergencies only. There is no playing around with a fire engine. It is a serious moment whenever you hear one or see one coming. I remember as a child every time my grandmother would hear a siren, she would stop and pray for the firefighters and the people they were helping. I have always done the same. My grandmother never told me I should pray, nor did she comment on it. I just saw her do it. Again, role modeling is the most effective way to teach positive behaviors.

One day I myself needed the assistance from the fire department. I came home one afternoon to find my house full of smoke, like a fog. You could barely see where you were walking. I could not, however detect any fire. I looked frantically. I checked every possible place but couldn't find the source of the fire. Finally I called the fire department stating that I felt silly calling because I did not think there could be a fire.

The dispatcher said they could send out a man. Yes, she said a man, meaning one man. A "man" does not mean 3 fire trucks, 2 paramedic vehicles, and a police officer. But here they came, sirens going, horns honking, and 3 fire trucks from 3 different fire departments! They were only supposed to send out 1 man with a special camera that could view the interior of the walls.

So here they are and by the way, so is my entire neighborhood. Everybody is out on the street wondering what house is burning to the ground. The fire fighters look in the walls. They look in my closets (that was embarrassing). They look in the fireplace, the stove, and yes finally the source of this 911 emergency call, a melted plastic Tommee Tippee cup lid in the dishwasher.

You know the old saying about "where there is smoke, there is fire?" That is not always true. How does this relate to self-esteem? How many times do we make an emergency out of something simple? Have you ever overreacted to an event in your child's life? How many times do we call 911 when it is a problem, not an emergency?

Don't make a huge deal out of an insignificant event. If your child makes a B on a project, don't make her feel guilty for it not being an A. Deal with what needs attention in a calm, less emotional way. Begin shifting from emotion into intellect.

Try to stay calm during stressful times. Avoid screaming, lecturing, and yelling hurtful words. The temptation is always there. If you are able to remain composed, your child's focus will be on their behavior not on your temper.

Some children actually enjoy seeing their parents or stepparents "lose it." Children often feed off of negative attention. It is as if they are saying, "See! I can control your behavior but you can't control mine!" Too often that is true. Do you want to know why the children or stepchildren can push your buttons so easily? They installed them!

Not only is your verbal response critical to your child's self-esteem, but it is also how you deliver the information. Many times I have suggested to parents that perhaps the content of their message is healthy and appropriate, but their delivery needs a little work.

When I want to make an impression on my children, I begin to speak so quietly that they can barely hear me. Particularly if I'm upset with them, I'll do so just to ensure that I remain calm. The famous line in our household that my children detested when they were little was, "I'm sorry that you are unhappy with your consequence because of the decision you made." They walked away and probably plotted our demise.

Kids Need You to Be the Parent

As parents, we are not called to become friends with our children. Of course we would prefer our children like us rather than not, but your children need a parent, not another buddy. Your children are not going to like much of what you do until they have their own children. You will then become a genius. But this accolade takes a very long time to arrive.

When you need to correct your child, do it with love. You can make a statement to your child without humiliating or shaming her. I'm not advocating that when your teen makes a bad decision that you just pat her head and tell her, "Oh you poor thing. I know you didn't mean to." Treat each offense or occurrence with the appropriate level of response.

A teenager who comes home from a party intoxicated or high should expect the fire engine to make a house call. Such behavior requires a severe consequence. Sadly because many parents made mistakes as teenagers, they feel it would be hypocritical to issue a consequence. This is a huge mistake.

I see this frequently in my office. Parents catch their teen drinking or smoking pot. They want to be understanding, forgiving, and merciful because it is a first offense. Guess what? It may be the first time he got caught, but it is rarely the first time it occurred. Treat it very seriously. Then drug test your child frequently afterward. Even if you believe your teen only drank or smoked pot one time, still drug test frequently.

As parents sometimes though, we treat every situation like it is an emergency. Some parents may not have the problem of rescuing, or dealing with issues as they present themselves. You may have the problem of calling for the fire engine when only a candle is burning. If your child is generally making good decisions with regards to being responsible, then celebrate! You are very blessed. There will be situations arise that prove to you however, that your child is not perfect. Don't be alarmed. Treat each situation with the level of appropriate reaction.

Needs Improvement

When I was in 8th grade, I kept getting "Needs Improvement" in the Conduct Department on my report card. I enjoyed talking when I should have been listening. My mother was tired of me entertaining in class when I should have been paying attention. She warned me that I better not come home with a "Needs

Improvement" again. She said, "I don't care what you have to do or what lengths you have to go to, change your conduct grade to a 'Satisfactory' or else!"

Well I knew my mother to be a person of her word. Being the obedient child I was, I took her literally. So, the next day in Math I march up to the teacher and ask to look at my grades. He handed me the grade book. I take my pencil and erase the N and made it into an S. I don't think my teacher noticed and I really didn't point it out to him. My mother said, "Do whatever it takes to change your grade." For me it took an eraser!

Had I been caught I had already established my defense. I did exactly what the woman said to do. After all I was only a child and thought my mother meant what she said. Fortunately on report card day, the evidence revealed that I had worked very hard to improve my conduct grade. I got a big, fat Satisfactory. My mother was very proud of me and bought me a new purse.

Should I have been dragged into therapy for committing such an illegal offense? Should my mother have called 911 for the fire truck to come had she known? Probably not, and I never did it again!

Many times I have had parents bring a child into therapy for an upsetting situation. Although it is better safe than sorry, often the situation was a normal part of growing up. The child didn't need psychotherapy, but the parents needed reassurance. Sometimes kids are just being kids and experiencing a normal part of their developmental process. I know as a parent of 3, that I have definitely overreacted and called 911 when it was not called for.

Staying calm and listening to your children without interruption can prevent unwanted emergency calls. If you call 911 for every little problem, the Fire Department usually begins to fine you for false alarms, and they put your name in the paper. These are all things I try to avoid.

Box Talks

Journal Time

1. When was the last time you rescued your child? Was it the best choice? Or did it perpetuate irresponsibility? What could you do differently the next time a similar situation arises?

2. How does your child do at making his bed or preparing food? Do you allow him to do so on his own, or do you go back and "fix it" to be perfect?

3. Ponder the lunch money example a few pages back. How did you feel about it? Is there a similar scenario in your home? What could

you do next time to encourage responsibility without rescue?

Family Time

1. Sit down with your family and work on a behavioral contract outlining specific expectations. Write down both the desired behavior and the consequence if the desired behavior is not met. For example: Write down that your child needs to pack his backpack every night. This includes any books, notes or homework due. The potential consequence is that if your child fails to do this and calls you to bring a forgotten item, you do not bring it. Then your child has the natural consequence of the missed work, and perhaps afterschool tutoring. Write down all chores, behaviors and attitudes. This builds self-confidence because children do better when they know exactly what is expected from them. Having it written down makes it more real for the child and parents. When I do a family behavioral contract in my office I have everybody sign it as though it is a legal document. Usually the kids do very well with the contract. It is the parents who struggle with consistency. It takes effort to reinforce the agreement daily when you're tired after a long day. Stick with it and

you'll experience long-lasting results in all the family members. I even have the parents commit to what they will work on too. The kids love this part and they get excited about the contract. For example, Mom's desired behavior may be to eliminate yelling or screaming (not that any of us have ever done that.) Her consequence might be to put $5.00 in The Fun Jar for everyone to go out and have frozen yogurt.

2. Reward your child when you see new behaviors that indicate progress with regards to responsibility. Verbally praise your child and really make her feel special. Also allow your child to pick a fun activity that you can enjoy together to show her how proud you are that she is making more mature choices. You can even have her pick out a new shirt if she needs one. Rewards, however, do not have to include getting a present. I just happen to really like presents!

CHAPTER 3

Battleship®

"Don't fight a battle if you don't
gain anything by winning."
— ERWIN ROMMEL

WHEN SHE WALKED IN my office, she presented as a very bright high school student struggling with self-mutilation (cutting) and suicidal thoughts. Her parents were extremely worried and desperate for help. When the family began counseling, the daughter was enrolled in four Advanced Placement classes in school and felt overwhelmed and embarrassed that she was unable to cope with her life and schedule. Her parents had no idea the pressure she was under. I advised the family to reduce the daughter's stress level by reevaluating her course load. Her parents agreed to

53

"pick their battles" and allowed her to change some of her classes back to regular courses. Soon the cutting and suicidal thoughts dissipated.

❖   ❖   ❖

Battleship®
Battleship® is a popular board game that has been around since 1967 with many different gaming systems now offering it on their platform. This game is in the toy box for the simple reason that parents need to pick their battles with their beloved offspring. You can literally be fighting about something every day. Those kids you wanted to have so badly when you were younger now provide daily, often hourly opportunities for you to suit up in your battle fatigues and go to war.

This chapter could begin and end with one sentence and it would be enough.

Pick your battles.

It would be the shortest chapter in history perhaps but clear to the point. Do you really want to get into a big, nasty fight over an issue that is not really worth it? No. So you are going to have to decide what is really important and what is not that big of a deal. Or the fighting won't end and no one will feel good about themselves in your home. Parents and children can impact each other's self-esteem in both positive and negative ways during times of peace and adversity.

Pray for God to help you know which battles to enter. Gary and Carrie Oliver make a very profound discovery in their book, *Raising Sons and Loving It!* "We don't want to belabor the point-but it deserves repeating yet again: every couple we interviewed who raised boys who now live for Jesus believed that prayer was the key to their parenting success."[5] Prayer is the key to success in every area of life. It's essential to pray for discernment over what conflict to battle over.

Remember back to the last time your daughter looked you up and down with a disgusted look on her face and said, "You think you look good in that?" Mothers, we are no better. We give disapproving looks with unsolicited comments, shattering little one's self-esteem countless times.

Your daughter may stroll in the kitchen for break-fast having just straightened her hair, and you casually remark how pretty her hair looks when it's curly. You just unknowingly entered into battle, crushed her self-esteem and insured she will never again wear her hair curly 'til death does she part.

So pick your battles. Make sure that you're building your child up rather than sinking a battleship. It may be fun to win a game. Oftentimes, however, it is not worth the cost of the ship destroyed. Psalm 55:18 states, "He redeems my soul in safety from the battle that I wage, for many are arrayed against me."

Fudgsicles® for Bullies

As a 5th grader the biggest battle I chose to engage in was a war against two bullies who happened to be brothers. These juvenile delinquents were feared by every kid in our zip code. They committed more crimes than I can even list. By the end of summer my sister Cindi and I had had enough! Every time the ice cream truck came on our street, we were thrilled to rush up and buy two of our favorite ice cream treats—Fudgsicles®. It never failed that the Hoodlum Brothers would chase us down and steal our confectionary chocolate treats right out of our hand, all the while bragging about how tough and bad they were.

The battle ensued. We decided to get even and make our own version of our Fudgsicle® treats. We got a bowl of wet mud and lovingly shaped it into frozen imitation Fudgsicle® bars, complete with wrapper and wooden stick. We then patiently waited for the sound of the truck.

It was late in the afternoon on a hot August day when the beautiful music emerged from the ice cream truck. We ran out to get in line so it looked like we were buying our usual, with the "Mudsicles" hidden beneath our shirts. After leaving the line we took the muddy treat out of the wrapper and lo and behold, here come the brothers. They swiped the "Mudsicles" out of our hands yelling, "You stupid girls! Thanks for the Fudgsicles® again." As they took a big bite of frozen mud delight, we yelled, "You're welcome!" and ran as fast as we could into our house.

They never bothered us again. They didn't know what we would do next; neither did we! You can only push a girl so far.

What is the moral of the story? Pick your battles and wear good running shoes. If something is important then go to battle, if not then live in peace. There is great wisdom in discerning what to let go of versus what to deal with. You certainly don't want to be a doormat or a pushover. With regards to parenting determine if it is a lesson necessary for life.

> ### *Don't Sink Your Battleship® for This:*
>
> 1. *Making a B on a paper or test.*
> 2. *Carrying a joke too far. (Obviously I have tremendous empathy for this poor soul!)*
> 3. *Occasionally their room not being picked up.*
> 4. *Sibling rivalry—let them work it out if possible.*
> 5. *Occasionally forgetting a chore.*

Suit Up For Battle

If your teenager comes in 30 minutes late from his curfew, you should absolutely deal with such. He needs to respect rules of authority. He needs to be on time for school and work. He needs to honor boundaries set for him. So, the very first time it happens there should be a consequence. No lectures of "If this happens again, you are in trouble." No warnings and no threats because he knew he was gambling with his freedom when he chose to be late.

Likewise when your child disregards rules and boundaries set for electronic privileges (i.e. video games, computer games, etc.), you need to be consistent and strong in enforcing issued rules. One infraction and the game or computer is confiscated. My suggestion is either no gaming during the school week or one hour of gaming after all homework is completed. Doing well on tests and projects may earn the child extra weekend time for playing.

Whatever amount you decide is appropriate for weekend playing, stick with the plan. Just be aware of what your child is doing with his time. It is too easy to waste eight hours playing, not realizing so much time has passed. Refuse to get into an argument about what guidelines you have set up. I have found that locking up gaming systems stops conflicts if you let him know he can't get it back until he's no longer fighting with you.

Always give a consequence the first time a rule is broken, no exceptions, no excuses are accepted. Be a person of your word 100 percent of the time. Teens in my office tell me all the time that not obeying the rules is simply a gamble. Your child should know it is a gamble and a battle he will always lose. It won't be you who sunk his battleship; he will have sunk it himself.

Box Talks

Journal Time

1. Reflect back on your childhood. Did you have a bully? If so, who was it and how did you handle it? Write about that memory and how it affected you.

2. What are some areas in your home that bring about repeated battles? Write them down and ponder what is worth going to battle over and what may be an overreaction on your part.

3. What would be an appropriate response for some of the misbehavior that may come about in your home?

Family Time

1. You have to get the game of Battleship® in some format and play it as a family. It is a blast!

2. Play the game of Switching Roles. In therapy I've had family members do this, and it is both fun and insightful. You simply have the adults

and children switch roles. Mom and Dad become their offspring. Junior and Juniorette become Mom and Dad for the evening. Really get into the role. You will see how your family depicts you. They may find out a thing or two about how they are perceived.

CHAPTER 4

The Game of Sorry®

"If you're going to do something
tonight that you'll be sorry for
tomorrow morning, sleep late."

— HENNY YOUNGMAN

I WAS DOING MARRIAGE COUNSELING with a young
couple who had recently married. They were both
concerned that they were fighting so much since they
rarely, if ever, fought while dating. The biggest issue
that arose was that the husband would not apologize
when he was wrong or had hurt his wife's feelings, even
if it was obvious. It seemed like such an easy thing,
two very easy English words for one who claimed he
truly cared to repair his struggling marriage.

While working together we reviewed both of their family histories. As a young boy, the husband was never required to apologize. I don't mean "hardly ever." I mean *never*. When he did something wrong, he would refuse to admit fault, and his parents let it go and didn't require him to say "I'm sorry," nor did they give him consequences for his lack of remorse. Sadly, as an adult he was unable and unwilling to correct this issue, even when logically explained to him in counseling. Those two words would not come out of his mouth. Ultimately, the couple divorced.

❖   ❖   ❖

The Game of Sorry®
This chapter does not have the title it bears because it is the sorriest chapter in the book. It is actually one of the more important ones. When I was a child one of my favorite games to play was the Parker Brothers board game called Sorry®. The game can be played with 2–4 players. Each opponent has 4 play pieces. The goal is to make it all the way around the board and be safe at home base. Each player draws a card and it tells how many spaces to move the play piece. If a player lands on a space where another player's piece is, you get to send that player back to Start and yell, "Sorry!"

Playing Sorry®
My family played Sorry® all the time. Each of us played deeply motivated to send our opponents back to the

starting position, so we could say that coveted word. It was such sweet victory unless it was said to you. The only family that enjoyed playing Sorry® more than mine was a family from the television series, "The Carol Burnett Show." In my favorite episode, Eunice, played by Carol Burnett, begs her family to play the game. Harvey Korman portrays Ed, Eunice's dimwitted husband. Mama, played by Vicki Lawrence, was hilarious as the crotchety, bad tempered mother who tries to make everyone's life miserable.

Each of the three characters engage in the game. Their game starts out competitively with tempers flaring. The players are practically pulling each other's hair out. They are screaming, rude, sarcastic, and revengeful. I just watched the skit on YouTube and have never laughed more. Each round gets a little more spiteful, a little more abusive and tremendously loud. All the players aggressively scream, "Sorry!" with more revenge and hostility than the opponent before. By the end of their game, it was a hilarious disaster that only those three actors could have pulled off!

The game of Sorry® is a wonderful metaphor for life and certainly for parenting. Elton John was wrong when he sang those words on one of his hit songs: "Sorry seems to be the saddest word." Actually, a lack of saying "sorry" would be the saddest.

Parents, teach your children to apologize and make amends to others when they are wrong. Taking responsibility for mistakes is critical in maturing as an individual at any age. It takes courage for children to recognize when they make a wrong decision and then to go back and make amends.

It is often possible to force a child to apologize. It is more critical to train a child to voluntarily make amends without being prompted. How can you instill that quality in your children so it becomes part of them? What can you do to facilitate their ability to see the consequences of their action and experience true remorse?

The answer to both of those questions is both simple and difficult. You, as the parent have to role model how to apologize. Kids need to see parents in action. Children and teens need to witness heartfelt apologies, not the sarcastic, smirking, "Sorry!" like in the game. This is not a game. It is hard-core real life.

It cannot be stressed enough how important it is to implement the concept of apologizing and making amends into your family as soon as possible, or even sooner. Children need to experience apologies made to them and to other family members. It is even therapeutic for them to observe you apologizing to the family pet if you were unkind.

It's Just Three Words

Kids of all ages must see the adults in their life asking for forgiveness and expressing sorrow for offending or hurting a loved one. This concept of saying, "I am sorry," or lack of it has actually paid for the swimming pool in my backyard as my office is flooded with people who cannot or will not apologize. A lifetime void of apologies leaves behind a tragic repetitive legacy of broken relationships, as marriages end and families fracture.

You may be feeling something like this right now: "Whoa now, saying 'I'm sorry' leaves me too vulnerable. After all, I can't admit to my kids that I'm not perfect. Why admit mistakes? I've got to keep this act going as long as I can! I have this image of perfection that my children and especially my stepchildren believe, so I must keep living the lie. If I'm found out, I'll lose all respect and authority. I'll lose control and they'll never listen to me again."

Actually the opposite is true! If you can't admit when you are wrong (and *everyone* is wrong sometimes), then why should your children? Remember that popular parenting announcement, "Do as I say not as I do?" What happens in reality is exactly the opposite. Humans repeat what those around them do—even when they don't want to repeat it! Children imitate their surroundings. Ever heard yourself promise you would *never* behave in the ridiculous manner your parents used to behave?

Wipe Your Hands

My mom had these turquoise velvet towels that we were forbidden to use. I always thought how crazy can you be? You bought expensive towels that no one can use. They are just there to admire. Seriously? Who admires towels? It was insanity!

I am proud to announce I now have expensive velvet towels in one of my bathrooms that I too do not want anyone to use. They are there to make the bathroom pretty. If you come to my house, you may admire them because that is why they are there. Please do not use the towels. If you use the bathroom, after washing your hands please just wipe them on your pants or use a paper towel from the kitchen. Come on now—I know you have a story just like mine going on, it just doesn't involve towels. We imitate our surroundings even when we don't want to.

Maybe when you were a child, you never saw or heard apologies from your parents. You saw them fight but you never witnessed them making up. Apologizing may be more challenging for you to correct because you are imitating your surroundings. It is imperative that you learn to make amends so that you don't pass down to your children what was passed down to you. That is an inheritance you do not want.

In *The Power Of A Praying Parent*, Stormie Omartian writes, "Likewise, if my children argue with each other, I ask them to say 'I'm sorry' and 'I forgive you' to one another. Even if they don't wholeheartedly feel those things at the time, I know that what they say will eventually work its way into their soul."[6]

Babies learn to talk by listening to their parents. It starts there. They are constantly looking to Mom and Dad for how they should feel and behave. It is sending a mixed and confusing message when we want children to act in a way that we cannot or will not act. Saying, "Damn it Ashley, quit cussing!" is probably not going to be successful in stopping profanity in your home.

The Next Traffic Stop

Parents who model responsibility by apologizing and admitting fault are training their children for life. The majority of parents fall short in this area. Let's see how you measure up.

Remember the last time you received a traffic ticket from a police officer? Maybe you were going too fast or perhaps that yellow light just changed to red sooner than you anticipated. What was your immediate verbal response after you were handed that citation as you drove away?

Here are some choices:

1. "Stupid cop! Why doesn't he go arrest some real criminals instead of harassing law abiding, tax paying, honest citizens who are just trying to get to work on time to help others!"

2. "This is not fair! The speed limit is ridiculously low anyway! Besides, that cop wouldn't even have a job if my taxes didn't pay her salary. She should be stopping to thank me! Jerk!"

3. "Just my luck! The cops spot me on their way to the donut shop."

Or:

4. "As much as I hate to admit it, I did run that red light and I'm fortunate I didn't have an accident. I really need to be more careful. I am going to use this ticket as a wake up call to improve my driving."

If you have ever said the last choice, you are in a very small, if even existent minority. For the rest of us, it's humbling to ponder what our negative responses are teaching our kids, such as:

1. Nothing is my fault.

2. Everything is someone's fault.

3. Rules are for everyone except for me because I am special (my personal favorite).

4. No one has the right to correct me.

5. I should be able to do anything I want.

6. I do not have to respect authority if they haven't earned it.

These are not concepts children need to learn and emulate. In fact, you spend your entire life as a parent doing everything you can to instill the opposite. But it doesn't matter what you tell them. It matters what you show them.

So the next time you get a traffic ticket with your children in the car beware that you are on stage with an attentive audience. Step up to the podium, bring your PowerPoint presentation, attach the lapel microphone, organize your notes, and straighten your jacket because you are about to deliver the presentation of your life on Responsibility and Admitting Fault. You will either pass or fail. And believe me they are taking notes and recording it on their phone!

No One Likes Perfect People

Children are relieved to discover that adults make mistakes. Have you ever had a friend or relative who seemed to never make a mistake? It appeared as if everything he or she did was perfect. It can be intimidating to be around a person who never seems to be wrong. It can really make you feel like you are not measuring up. Kids feel the same way.

When I have heard sermons from church and the pastor reveals his own struggles and imperfections, it encourages me to be honest and real also. Why? Because it was role modeled. I do not walk back to my car judging his sins, thinking "Oh how terrible!" Rather I think, "Thank goodness he has the strength to be genuine and authentic." It encourages me to do the same.

It is difficult to have success in other areas of your life when you cannot say two simple words. As much as you may dislike this flaw in yourself, someone close to you dislikes it more. If you as an adult have never learned to apologize and ask for forgiveness, then quite possibly you were never expected to as a child. Perhaps you had parents who thought you never did anything wrong, and you foolishly bought into that and believed it. Please do not become that type of parent. You are damaging your child for life if you believe she never makes mistakes. If you get a phone call reporting that your child is picking on another child at school, don't immediately assume your child is innocent. Some kids are very good at manipulating their parents into believing they are victims when they are the ones doing the victimizing. Admitting fault is so relevant for healthy development.

Calling the Cops

As I've indicated, my sister and I loved to play practical jokes as children. We still do. Our neighbors down the street where we grew up never liked us much. They thought we were troublemakers. We were not troublemakers. We were creative and easily bored. One time when our God-fearing religious neighbors had a Bible study, we anonymously phoned the police saying there was a possibility that people in the house were smoking pot. Adults walked in with Bibles but you can never be sure.

A few moments after the police left, the homeowner came over beating on our door. He actually accused, without proof, that my sweet sister and I had called the police. My mother brought us in and asked us if we had committed the horrible crime. We felt guilty, stood up straight and said, "Mom we love Jesus. We would never want to break up a Bible study, and oh, by the way, what is pot?"

To this very day, my mother does not know the truth. Parents want to believe children are being honest. Parents, you can be easily manipulated because you may not want to know the truth.

When you get that bang on your front door, consider all your options.

Please Forgive Me

Often you need to say you are sorry even if you do not believe you are wrong. This can be extremely painful and may require Ibuprofen, but to live in peace, one may need to apologize. You can always say, "I am so sorry. I didn't realize that I hurt your feelings. That was never my intention. Please forgive me." Notice that this statement does not admit fault. You are merely apologizing that your words or deeds caused pain, and you are genuinely sorry it had that result even though you may not take back the message. This approach goes a lot farther in getting along than, "I didn't hurt your feelings. You are just being a baby and being overly sensitive like you always are."

It is better to live in peace. Be the peacemaker in your family. Romans 12:18 implores, "If possible, so far as it depends on you, live peaceably with all." Matthew 5:9 says, "Blessed are the peacemakers, for they shall be called sons of God."

You don't always have to be right. Besides you can always know in your head that you are right and just not say it out loud. At least that works for me.

When there is a basic refusal to ask for forgiveness and recognize self-fault, there is selfishness. Most of us are selfish enough already. That is one trait you really don't want magnified to your child. We teach our children both our good characteristics and our bad ones—you know the ones we try to cover up. The more covers you throw on an object, the bigger the object appears. Ever notice the words in your rearview mirror, "objects are closer than they appear?" Things you think you are hiding from your children are closer to them than they appear to you.

As a child, when you are hiding under the covers, you think no one can see you. However the more blankets you put on, the more obvious the object you are trying to hide. It is the same with our faults. Do whatever it takes to become the best "you" possible because there is a junior executive at your house getting on the job training right now. Quit playing the game of Sorry®, and turn it into real life in your home and in your relationships with your family. You'll win every time you say those precious words "I'm Sorry."

Box Talks

Journal Time

1. Reflect on your childhood. How was saying "I'm Sorry" handled when mistakes were made? Did your parents apologize? Whether they did or didn't, how did it affect you?

2. When was the last time someone said "I'm Sorry" to you? How did it affect your relationship?

3. Have you gotten a traffic ticket with your children in the car? How did you respond? How did your kids respond? Do you think you got graded "Pass" or "Fail"?

Family Time

1. Of course you have to play Sorry® with your kids as it is a fun and mandatory requirement.

2. Watch the Youtube video of the Carol Burnett Show where they are playing Sorry®.

3. Meet together as a family to discuss how important it is to make amends to each other.

CHAPTER 5

The Mirror

"Long-lasting change that will help you
create new habits and actions requires an
inside-out approach, as well as two very
important tools: the mirror and time."

— DARREN L. JOHNSON

I WAS COUNSELING WITH A WOMAN who detested her
appearance. Ironically, she was a natural beauty with
only one noticeable flaw, a rather large nose. She let
me know she had decided to have plastic surgery. She
was ready to fix the problem that had drawn ridicule
all through her school years. She was sick and tired
of the stares and jokes.

She had the surgery, and by the time the swell-
ing and bruising went away, she came in for one of

her sessions with me and not surprisingly, she was just beautiful. Anyone who saw her walking down the street would be convinced she was a model. But she did not see it. To her, there was no change. In the mirror and in her mind, she was the person everyone made fun of—an awkward, large-nosed joke of the school. Her nose got fixed, but her self-image had not changed. We had work to do.

❖   ❖   ❖

The Mirror

The next toy in the box is a toy mirror. We all played with it. Some of us still do. What reflections of yourself are you showing your children? What do the children in your family see you advertising about yourself? When someone compliments your hair, how do you respond? Do you reply with, "Oh it looks terrible, I was supposed to get it cut, and my hairdresser was sick!" Or do you react by saying, "Thank you."

Such a simple reply indicates to your children or stepchildren how you feel about yourself. Your response shows your children how they too should respond when complimented. It may sound like a real stretch to connect how you receive compliments to how you feel about yourself. It may particularly sound like a real stretch to link self-esteem with how you respond to a compliment about your hair. But think about how you feel when you're having a bad hair day! Sometimes you are just not aware that you have a long way to go yourself in having healthy self-esteem. You just need a wake up call.

I Don't Want to Ride the Space Shuttle

One summer, my family and I flew to Florida for a much-anticipated vacation. It was the first time to visit that beautiful state. Our three children were looking forward to all we had planned. They were excited about going to Disney World. They couldn't wait to see their favorite Disney characters and ride all the wonderful rides. The first few days, however, we were going to relax at the beach.

As we were on our way to Palm Beach the children were talking about the different rides at Disney World. As we drove along the highway, we noticed that many cars had pulled over and stopped on the side of the road. People were getting out of their cars and staring up at the sky.

We had no idea what was going on, so we stopped to investigate.

Families were lined up along the highway gazing up at the sky. We then learned that Cape Canaveral was preparing for a launch. We were thrilled to have this unexpected opportunity. None of us had seen a rocket launching into space except on television.

Suddenly, the rocket soared majestically into the clear, blue sky. The sight was utterly spectacular. It was also the loudest sound I had ever heard. Our two-and-a-half year-old daughter, who had been standing beside us, frantically began climbing up to her father's arms. She was holding on for dear life when she cried, "I don't want to ride that space shuttle!"

She assumed we were standing in line for a ride at Disney World. Sometimes you believe you are at your final destination when you still have a long way to go.

You may have just read this and thought, "This is all great for you but how can I help my child feel good about himself in the mirror when I find my own self-esteem doesn't exist when I look in the mirror! You just don't know what I've been though in my life."

If You Don't Own it, You Can't Sell It

You cannot teach what you do not possess. But you can take steps to become emotionally healthy yourself and build your own self-esteem. How do you do that? There are many ways. One option is counseling. Often times only a few sessions can help you achieve the results you desire. Many people have felt plagued with low self-esteem since childhood but have just lived with it. Therapy can be life changing. Other individuals may benefit from personal coaching. Hiring a life coach can be helpful in dealing with unwanted behaviors that impact your choices and how you feel about yourself.

Proverbs 11:14 states, "Where there is no guidance, a people falls, but in an abundance of counselors there is safety."

Attending motivational seminars can also be extremely helpful in changing and improving your self-esteem. It is encouraging to hear speakers who challenge you to strive for improvement and excellence. Learning new ways to live a more successful life— emotionally, physically, spiritually, financially, and relationally—helps build a stable self-worth and in turn, helps parents develop better parenting skills.

Reading inspirational books that facilitate positive change is another excellent way to improve how you feel about yourself. Hopefully, as you read this book you are realizing the worth you hold as a person. You are that much closer to passing down that inheritance to your children.

Becoming actively involved in a local church can also be a wonderful place to work on self-esteem. God can heal the wounds from the source of what has hurt you. Listening to sermons that inspire, encourage, and challenge can help you become the person you want to be.

God Can Repair Your Cracked Mirror

With God's guidance and grace, you have the ability to change any area where you are currently stuck. With God nothing is impossible. Yes, facing the mirror and learning to love the inner and outer you may not come easily. Growing towards self-love is sometimes uncomfortable, but so is living in a rut. You want to achieve healthy self-esteem, so you can teach your kids to have healthy self-esteem. It requires you get out of your uncomfortable ruts and move forward. And looking in the mirror and seeing someone lovely is a huge step. Learning to accept praise is another.

The people you know who graciously accept praise in a sincere way typically like who they are. Usually those people are confident, self-assured, and secure. Isn't that the ultimate goal for all of us as parents and stepparents? We want to raise those kinds of children that grow up to be those kinds of adults. Whether you are the biological parent, the stepparent, or both, the mirror you show those children creates a lifetime memory and example.

My oldest son was complimenting me one day because I "had such nice manners." I replied by saying, "Thank you honey but what prompted you to say that?" He said, "You are always praising us for our manners, so I thought I would do the same."

And now for a less flattering story. Some time ago, my family and I were waiting at a traffic light behind a car that had not realized the light had changed to green. All of a sudden my three children screamed from the top of their lungs, "GO PEOPLE!" I was appalled at their lack of patience and their abundance of rudeness, so I began lecturing them about tolerance. I was explaining that you can't lose your temper when life doesn't move as quickly as you think it should.

Immediately they all (including my dear husband) exclaimed, "You say that all the time!"

I could not believe that in addition to their rudeness and lack of patience, I had to include lying about their mother to their lists of faults. And for my husband to side with the band of liars was equally insulting. Traitor!

I truly did not believe any of my family's accusations and felt angry and resentful. Then one day, yes, you must know how this story is turning out, I was sitting at a traffic light that had turned green, when out of my very own mouth I heard, in a loud, bellowing voice that sounded like Satan himself, "GO PEOPLE!" Thank God I was alone.

Live the Example

We teach our children our good behaviors and teach them our bad behaviors even better. Modeling positive behavior and self-esteem needs to be evident for children. Parents are constantly being observed and studied. This happens continually with your own children and probably with greater scrutiny with stepchildren.

Why is that fair? It is not. It is also equally unjust as a stepparent to judge your stepchildren with greater scrutiny than your own children. Even "picking favorites" with biological children is damaging to all involved. Unfortunately, that old, "You're the adult" card gets played here, along with "You're supposed to be the mature one."

In counseling sessions, I have heard these statements more times than I could possibly count, "Why should I go out of my way to be nice to a kid who treats me as though he hates my guts?" "Why should I always have to be the one who reaches out to communicate?" Many parents and stepparents feel the only time they are ever treated with respect is when their child wants something.

Growing Up As the Parent

As a Christian and Godly parent, you are the example of what Jesus Christ is about. It is often very difficult to have to choose God's ways over our own selfish and controlling attitudes.

It is the responsibility and obligation of the parent to be the parent. Being childish and immature has no place in parenting. Take a deep breath and make the best decision you can whether it hurts you or not (and it will). Mirror for your children how you hope they will parent. Children may seem like they are not paying attention but they are. Kids are sponges, absorbing everything around them, both positive and negative. How you parent your children will affect generations. We are all living proof of that.

For many children in blended or traditional families, the only example of Christianity they may see is whom *you* see in the mirror. That is such a serious responsibility. It is one that can only be successfully accomplished with God's intervention. Pray that God gives you wisdom, discernment, love, and patience to make it through one conversation at a time with your children.

Why Not Pray?

Frequently, I have asked clients in counseling sessions if they pray for God's help regarding their problems. Approximately 90 percent of the responses are, "I never even thought about praying," and these are Christians I ask. We need all the help we can get. God is waiting for you to ask Him to intervene for your particular situation.

Too many times, however, we treat God like He is a magic genie we found in a lantern. You fear he will only grant you three wishes, so you better be careful that you don't ask Him to help you find your keys because POOF, now you only have two more wishes.

"So I say to you: Ask and it will be given to you; seek and you will find; knock and the door will be opened to you. For everyone who asks receives; the one who seeks finds; and to the one who knocks, the door will be opened." Luke 11:9-10 NIV

Too often people don't want to bother God with their needs because compared to others, their problems may seem insignificant. There will always be people with problems much worse than yours and others with problems not as severe as yours. Your difficulties will always be in the middle. You may not want to bother God, but He is waiting for the invitation.

God is Waiting for the Phone Call

God is bothered when we choose not to include Him when we are troubled with even the smallest of difficulties. It must sadden God when we refuse to go to Him in prayer with our issues. God wants to help you but He will not force His solutions onto you. If your teenager lost his keys, wouldn't you stop and try to help him find them? And yet, limits are imposed on God based on erroneous beliefs or previous religious training. God is interested in you, and He loves you.

He cares about your struggles, your pain, your issues, and even your keys.

Matthew 7:11 says: "If you then, who are evil, know how to give good gifts to your children, how much more will your Father who is in heaven give good things to those who ask him!"

Again, He cares about your keys and everything else about you and your life that is lost. Jesus died on the cross for our sins. I believe that Jesus may be telling us something like this:

> You don't want to bother Me? I was beaten with a whip and flogged and crucified. I bore all sickness and disease on the cross so that you could receive healing. Yet you don't want to bother My Heavenly Father with a request for healing? You don't want to bother Me?

Jesus won the lottery ticket for you, and you won't cash in the ticket. God desires to heal you, your family, and your children in every area. This includes emotionally, physically, spiritually, financially and in your relationships. You may be looking in the mirror thinking about all the mistakes you've made. You may feel that you've done this to yourself. How can you ask God to fix something when you created the problem? Many problems people have are a result of poor decisions they made. If you are only going to let God help you with problems that you had nothing to do with creating, then He won't be helping you at all. You must forgive yourself and move on. You are not helping anyone by choosing to hold on to the past. Get free.

Often times the wounds from our childhood make it difficult to move on, difficult, but not impossible. Think about the most damaging thing as a child that negatively impacted how you felt about yourself. Mine would have to be having a severe case of acne.

Avoiding the Mirror

I had it for 10 long years. That is a decade. It felt like an eternity. I absolutely hated the mirror. I would go to the mall and practically run through the cosmetic department hoping to avoid the women who worked there. Sadly, one of them always managed to catch me.

"Oh honey," it always started, "You have pimples all over your face. You poor thing! You have a horrible complexion. You'd be such a pretty girl if your face ever clears up." Then they would try to sell me some wonder product that would turn me into Miss America.

I was on antibiotics for 10 years and was nauseated everyday from them, had my face chemically peeled, had it burned with dry ice and had injections into the actual blemish. The only cream I wanted was vanishing cream. I never thought it was possible to have any self-esteem until I moved on. I rose above the problem and thanked God everyday for healing my skin in faith. And today it is a miracle that I will even walk into a department store, but unfortunately I have been totally cured from that too.

For many years after my skin was clear, if anyone ever complimented me, I thought they were making fun of me. The invisible scars of low self-esteem can last longer than any visible scars from acne. Even through the tumultuous adolescent years, I tried not to allow the hurtful comments from others to affect how I felt about myself. I tried to find other qualities within me to focus on that were positive. And it worked! Don't allow others to negatively affect your self-esteem. You have a choice on how you react to negative input.

Joyce Meyer writes in *Battlefield of the Mind for Teens*, "Life isn't easy, but it is simple. Positive minds produce positive lives. Negative minds produce negative lives. And positive minds are always filled with faith and hope, while negative minds are full of fear and doubt."[7]

Do not give anyone permission to rob you of your self-worth. No one has that right. When you relinquish your power to another individual and that person continually damages your self-esteem then you are in essence, choosing to destroy yourself. No human should have that much power over your life.

Speaking Positively

Take back your power and take back your self-esteem. Learn to love whom you see in the mirror because you are teaching your children to do the same. When they hear you belittle yourself and put yourself down, your children think that is what they are supposed to do.

They think it is just good manners to be self-deprecating. *After all, you don't want to feel too good about yourself or you will look conceited.* So they learn they should feel badly about themselves instead. And self-deprecation becomes the habit, and low self-esteem follows.

You would be amazed how challenging it is for people to even acknowledge their own *positive* qualities. Yet it is such a vital step for anyone to build self-confidence. I want you to try it now for yourself. Take a few moments to write down 10 positive characteristics about yourself. Stop! Don't read anymore. Write them down.

How did you feel while you were listing your positive qualities? Did you feel embarrassed? Did you feel like you were bragging about yourself? Are you afraid someone might see your list?

If you were asked to write down 10 of your negative characteristics, NO PROBLEM! You would be writing faster than you could think. After all, it is just not godly to think too highly of ourselves. No it is not, and it also is not godly to see yourself as the low-life loser piece of scum that Satan has been trying to convince you of your whole life. So begin accepting and acknowledging your positive traits that you possess. You do have some. I promise.

The Positive List

During counseling sessions, I tell clients to write down as many positive things as they can think of about themselves. They are to bring the positive list back to their next appointment. At least 50% of the clients return in a week with a negative not a positive list. I am extremely clear about the assignment. It is as though some individual's brains won't hear and accept the positive.

What does this have to do with your child? Again, you cannot teach a concept that you know nothing about. You cannot teach your child to tie his shoe if you don't know how to tie your own. Of all the people you know and admire in the world, whom would you choose to be? If you picked anyone other than yourself, then you have a problem with your own self-esteem. How do you bless your child with a healthy self-image? Get one yourself!

Arrogant or Insecure?

A friend of mine held a dinner party where the date of one of the guests literally flung his coat at her without so much as a "Hello, nice to meet you," when my friend opened her door. Later, the man realized his mistake, apologized, and told her he thought she was the servant.

This was not a man with healthy self-esteem, although many would argue that he felt too good about himself. Conceit and arrogance are found in people who do not possess true self-esteem. Their value of worth is found in possessions and attainments, not in who they are as a person.

I was watching a rerun of the old sitcom called MASH recently on television. Captain Pierce (Alan

Alda) was giving a very long oral delivery. Finally, he said, "Well enough of talking about me. Let's talk about you for a change. What do you think of me?"

Low self-esteem can disguise itself well. Think of all the people you know who until now, looked arrogant and self-absorbed. In reality, they are probably insecure and fearful that someone will discover the truth about them. Many successful and well-known people have told me that their number one fear is that someone will find out that they don't know what they're doing. It is a common fear.

People lack self-esteem because they operate in fear.

1. You may be afraid that someone was right when you were told how worthless you are.

2. You may be afraid that you are not good enough.

3. You may be afraid that someone is better than you.

4. You may fear being abandoned.

5. You may fear that you'll be fired

And what if none of those things are true and never happen? After all, almost everything you worry about never comes to pass. You've wasted a lifetime worrying about something imagined. Rise above fear. 2 Timothy 1:17 says, "For God gave us a spirit not of fear but of power and love and self-control."

Overcoming Fear

Fear is not from God. It is impossible to operate in fear and faith at the same time. Overcome fear and you will overcome the obstacles that chip away at your self-esteem. God wants to heal your self-esteem. He wants you to feel good about yourself in the same way that you want for your child.

I believe when we get to heaven that God is going to reveal all of the opportunities we had to include Him in the solution of every problem. We are limiting God by assuming that He is only powerful enough to answer the big difficulties. He is God. He created multi-tasking. He multi-tasks continually. He can assist you with the location of your keys while working on world peace at the same time. It would seem to be insulting to God that we as parents want to help our children with their problems, while believing God to be too busy to help us with ours.

God Doesn't Like Genie Lamps

Get God out of the genie lamp you've had Him in. You will be amazed at His ability to transform you and your situation. Begin to feel hopeful about the possibilities that could occur in your family. Begin to feel more positively about yourself. You have tremendous ability and potential. Stop verbalizing negative statements about yourself because you are training your child to do the same. Put yourself into success minded thinking.

In the mirror, see yourself free from the past. See your potential. See yourself as God sees you. See a parent with healthy self-esteem and confidence, so you can show that image to the children in your home. You cannot sell a concept to a child that you do not already own.

In the mirror become and see the person that you want your child to be.

Be real. Be authentic. If you are smoking a cigarette but lecturing him on the evils of tobacco, buy an extra pack the next time you are at the store. Your child will eventually need them. Instead, become the best version of yourself that you can possibly become. Your child doesn't need a lecture from you. He needs a living example. He needs you to act out how to live life successfully.

Box Talks

Journal Time

1. Earlier in the chapter, I asked you to write down 10 positive traits YOU have. Pull out that list (or write it out now if you forgot to write it). We all have positive qualities. Recognize your own.

2. Go to a mirror and look into your face and eyes for five minutes. Just sit with yourself in front of the mirror. Then write in your journal how you felt. Did you see someone you love?

3. Write about your self-esteem during your childhood. Did you experience any challenge as I did with acne? What was it, and how did it affect you?

Family Time

1. Gather the family together at dinner or a convenient time and ask each of your family members to share 10 things they like about themselves. (You've already done this for yourself, so you are ready to go).

2. Each family member develops a quiz about himself consisting of 5–10 questions. The questions can range in level of difficulty. For example, "A Quiz about Amy" might have "What is my favorite movie?" Or "What do I want to be when I grow up?" Make copies of the questions for every family member. If there are 4 family members then each member develops a quiz. Each member will then answer 3 quizzes. See who gets the best grade and knows each member the best.

3. Find pictures of each member when you were little kids, even the parents. Get your picture and talk about what you remember at that age. What were your adventures, hopes, and dreams?

CHAPTER 6

Silly String®

"Silly String® has served me well
in Combat especially in looking for
IADs, simply put, booby traps."

— FORMER MARINE BRUCE SCHNEIER

~

DURING RUSH HOUR TRAFFIC one evening a man was being tailgated by an extremely high-strung, stressed-out lady. When he approached an intersection, the light suddenly turned yellow. He chose to brake rather than trying to beat the red light. The tailgating woman began honking, screaming, and threatening the man. She was so furious that she had not made it through the intersection.

While she was still ranting, she heard a tap on her window. It was a very serious looking police officer. The officer ordered her to vacate her vehicle with her hands up. He then drove her in his car to the police station where she was searched, fingerprinted, photographed, and then placed her in a holding cell.

After many hours, a policeman entered the woman's cell and escorted her back to the booking desk. She was then given her personal belongings as the officer then told her, "I am so very sorry for this horrible mistake! You see I pulled up behind your car while you were blowing your horn, screaming profanities and flipping off the man in front of you. I noticed the 'Choose Life' license plate holder, the 'What Would Jesus Do' bumper sticker, the 'Follow Me to Sunday School' bumper sticker, and the chrome-plated Christian fish emblem on the trunk. Naturally, I assumed you stole the car."

❖   ❖   ❖

Silly String®

Many of us are advertising one thing and living quite another, just like the irate driver. Our children see it all. Strive to portray healthy responses to stressful events. Stress will always be lurking around the corner. There are often days filled with pressures and troubles. One of the best ways to deal with problems is through the appropriate use of humor. Laughter releases stress. The benefits of laughter reach far beyond the obvious.

When daily life delivers stress, what better relief than laughter? And what better avenue for laughter than good ole Silly String®? I have loved Silly String® since it first came out in the 70's. It saved me from being bored countless times and now learning it has saved actual lives in the military brings me joy. Silly String® is amazing. It is one of the most important novelty toys available in facilitating self-esteem in your family. Why? Silly String® is probably the only toy in the box where there is laughter 100 percent of the time. It is impossible to have a Silly String® fight with your children without laughter and fun. Whether you are part of the action or just part of the audience, it delivers laughter. No matter the age of your family—from preschool to senior citizens— Silly String® fights encourage entertainment, amusement, and humor.

When you play with Silly String®, you turn into who you used to be. Remember when you were fun and adventurous? You used to care more about having a good time than whether you had pink Silly String® remnants in your front yard. You are still in there somewhere.

Finding Humor

One of the strongest assets found in individuals with a healthy self-image is an ability to laugh and find humor in life. Life can be so serious because life *is* serious. Parents need to model healthy reactions to stress, and incorporating humor is often a healthy coping mechanism. It helps you disengage from stress in a healthy way. Robert Orben once said, "The world

now has so many problems that if Moses had come down from Mount Sinai today, the two tablets he'd carry would have been aspirin!"[8]

"Perhaps I know why it is man alone who laughs: He alone suffers so deeply that he had to invent laughter,"[9] said Friedrich Nietzsche many years ago. Laughter can relieve our pain and heal our hurts. A person with a healthy self-image is able to find humor in the most difficult of times.

When you have a difficult day, what messages are you conveying to your children or family? Do you come home in a bad mood? Do your children disappear after they see the look on your face? Do you enter your home complaining, griping, and blaming the world for your complicated day? You are illustrating how your child should react when he or she has a rough day on the playground or in the classroom. If your child regularly brings home a negative report of the day's events, take a look at your own daily report. You may find similarities.

Benefits of Laughter

Job 8:21 says, "He will yet fill your mouth with laughter, and your lips with shouting." In *How Laughter Works*, Marshall Brain says, "Laughter reduces levels of certain stress hormones. In doing this, laughter provides a safety valve that shuts off the flow of stress hormones and the fight-or-flight compounds that swing into action in our bodies when we experience stress, anger or hostility."[10]

Laughter is essential for healthy living and healthy families. Lifelong comedians, Bob Hope and George Burns both lived to be 100 years old. Laughing and providing humor for others can have enormous positive effects even on our health and outlook. As the psalmist says, "Then our mouth was filled with laughter, and our tongue with shouts of joy;" Psalm 126:2.

It is very enjoyable to associate and engage in conversations with funny people. You can actually teach your children how to incorporate humor into their daily life. Buy joke books. Play practical jokes on each other that are funny but not hurtful for anyone. If you look at my counseling website you will see my only hobby listed: "playing practical jokes on those I love."

The rule of appropriate humor is to only make fun of yourself, never anyone else. Humor and laughter should never hurt anyone's feelings, but rather it should be positive and creative. Besides, it is a wonderful character trait to learn to laugh at oneself at the moment something embarrassing happens (you'll laugh later, so why not at the moment it happens when everyone else is laughing). There is a difference between being self-deprecating and making one-self the object of humor. Self-deprecation attacks one's self-worth. Making oneself the object of humor is laughing at human mistakes and embarrassing events that were unexpected.

Happy Birthday

For my birthday one year, my friends connected a rope between trees across my lawn. On the rope were several bras, which were size 50 DDDDD filled with balloons. There were also multiple pairs of huge granny panties that my whole family could have fit in together. To finish off the lovely decorations was a gigantic sign that read, "Happy 50th!"

I was, however not even close to 50! Many people throughout the week congratulated me on turning 50. I live on a busy road. Some seemed surprised I was that old, at least I hoped they were surprised. No matter how convincingly I tried to explain to others how I was not really 50, nobody believed me. Friends would say, "You don't have to be defensive about turning 50! Don't worry about it."

What my children learned from this was how much fun it can be to play lighthearted, appropriate practical jokes on friends. Although I am skeptical that placing large underwear in my yard was appropriate, I have to admit it was really funny. And I have no doubt that it was a blast for my "trespassing" friends.

My children have become much more creative and funny just thinking of new ways to make others laugh. Creating an elaborate scheme for a hilarious practical joke is a common occurrence in our home today just as it was in the home I grew up in as a child. As I relayed earlier, my sister and I were well-known notorious practical jokers during our childhood and adolescent years, well actually through the current date.

Paging My Mother

When my mother, sister, and I would go to the mall, we rarely shopped at any department store that we didn't find a way to laugh and have fun. After all, shopping can be monotonous if you don't throw in a few surprises. One day my sister and I snuck off from Mom and spoke to Customer Service, where they frantically made an emergency announcement through the store's paging system.

> Attention all shoppers! We have an emergency situation! There is a lost mentally challenged adult. She is blond, has green eyes and is wearing a black pantsuit and answers to the name of Joy. She appears normal but becomes agitated and angry very easily. She may be in the Sportswear Department. If you locate her, please don't scare her. Her daughters will be there immediately to take care of her.

You can understand how this was much more fun than the usual shopping experience. Although our antics usually affected the amount of purchases we were able to get, the look on our mother's face was better than any pair of jeans I wanted. Besides, the jeans would be worn out by now, but this story isn't and still makes me laugh.

My three children were spending the week at my sister's house in Oklahoma one summer. My youngest son had a very loose tooth when they left and I was worried about him losing it in Oklahoma. Apparently I had very good reason to worry. When I got my children back home, I found out that he had indeed lost the tooth while at my sister's. He handed me a letter that he found under his pillow in Oklahoma that said this:

> This is the Tooth Fairy in Oklahoma! Congratulations on losing your first tooth. I only give a quarter in Oklahoma for each tooth, however if you will put this letter under your pillow in Texas, the Texas Tooth Fairy will give you $20.00. Everything is bigger and better in Texas.
>
> —Signed: Oklahoma Tooth Fairy

So of course I had to put $20.00 under his pillow that night and $20.00 under his pillow every time he loses a tooth for the rest of his life! Not a very practical joke I would say because the kid had a lot of teeth.

Hearing Voices

We need to laugh. We need a sense of humor in the midst of life's daily stress. Make it a habit to look for a way to use amusement to bless a loved one every day. You can find humor at any time, in any situation. For example, recently my family went to lunch together, but we met in two separate cars. I was going home with the kids while my husband stopped at the grocery store. I really had not planned on hiding his truck from where he parked it in the lot but something just came over me. It was as though a voice said, "There is his truck right there and you have a key to it. You have an obligation to provide laughter to your humor-deprived children."

Laughed we did, so hard that we were crying. We moved his truck completely to another parking lot. We positioned my car strategically so we are not spotted. He walks out with 2 huge sacks of groceries. In my defense, I thought he was only picking up one item. It actually made it funnier.

He walks to the spot where he thought he parked and another car was there. He looks so adorably baffled and confused. He walks up and down every row twice. Once he stopped and looked at the sky. I guess he was praying. We loved that part. We are squealing and laughing so intensely that we cannot even speak. Then finally he remembers he is married to me. He calls my cell phone and says, "What did you do with my truck?" I was insulted that he automatically assumed I had moved it when it could have been stolen. Crime is at an all-time high.

People ask me all the time, "Aren't you scared you'll make the people you prank mad?"

I am scared beyond belief. My husband is my dentist, and I was scared to see him professionally for quite some time! You don't want to make your dentist mad as I no longer have a key to his truck.

A Lesson Not Soon Forgotten

In high school, I was always looking for new, innovative ways to escape potential boredom in Haltom City. In Ron Hall and Denver Moore's book, *Same Kind of Different as Me,* Ron Hall also a native of Haltom City, Texas describes our prior mutual zip code as "a town so ugly that it was the only one in Texas with no picture postcard of itself for sale in the local pharmacy."[11] Haltom City may not have been Hollywood, but it saw a lot of stunts as long as I lived there.

As a child, my mother embraced humor and laughter in our home. She pulled a few practical jokes herself, and one she played on me is still my number one favorite. The summer of my 17th year was apparently boring for me. I needed a little hilarity and had already seen all the funny movies. I talked a few friends into going to buy water guns to see what kind of fun we could create.

I was the driver. The part I played was to appear lost and get the good Samaritans to roll down their window at the traffic light. As I asked for directions to the local police station (ironic, I know) their window was rolled completely down. We then all shot our water guns right into the poor, unsuspecting driver's face. It was not always a hit. People just don't have a sense of humor it seems. I bragged to everyone I knew about how I had never been caught doing this watergun prank. We came close, but we always got away. Then one afternoon, the doorbell rings. I peek out between the curtains and see it is the police! So I run like the scared chicken I still am and hide under my bed. I'm praying like I never have before. "God if you get me out of this one, I will never play another practical joke again!" (Well I didn't really plan to keep *that* promise.)

Next, my traitor of a mother brings the officer into my bedroom, pulls up the bedspread and shows him where I'm hiding. I thought I was going to die or worse, be carted off to jail. Then I hear a big, "Gotcha!" I look up at the officer's face, and it's my friend's father who borrowed the uniform. He too enjoyed an occasional practical joke. My mother planned the whole thing. She had been telling me all summer to stop the water gun crimes, and finally she had found a way to enforce it. I never did it again.

Humor can most always help get you through stressful situations. On a coffee mug the other day I saw imprinted, "A woman is like a tea bag, you'll never know how strong she is until she's in hot water."

Just Plane Stressed

On a flight home from Orlando, I noticed a lady who could have used the coping skills of humor. She was frantically threatening her 3-year-old son while they were boarding the plane. She wanted him to sit in the middle seat while she sat on the aisle seat. He protested loud enough for the pilot and the rest of the plane to hear, "No mommy I don't want to sit by a stranger. You sit there. She looks mean".

The mother starts enunciating her words very precisely, as she threatens in a loud intimidating way to this sweet and scared child. "You better sit there now, or I'm taking you off this plane and leaving you all by yourself in Orlando."

Crying loudly he begs, "Please Mommy why can't YOU sit there."

"Because I'm too fat to sit in the middle," she snaps.

Realizing the futility of asking again, the boy reluctantly settles in next to the mean looking stranger.

"Mommy," he asked.

"Yes," she responded.

"Why are you fat?" he questioned.

It was all me and the rest of the passengers could do to contain our laughter. As parents, we constantly make mistakes, especially when tired and stressed. However, threatening children with impossible consequences only teaches them you are not a person of your word. That 3-year-old may not have known that his mother was bluffing, but he soon will. Never threaten your children with a consequence that you are unwilling to carry out. All it does is teach children and teens that you are not trustworthy. And that is definitely not a lesson you want learned.

Coping Skills

Stress management is one of the biggest areas I treat in my practice. Everybody needs to find ways to deal with stress, as it is a regular part of life for all ages. I teach my clients that laughter can be a huge stress reducer, plus it helps you feel better. Even in the most adverse situations you can still find opportunities to laugh. Start teaching coping skills, including the use of humor, to your children while they are young. Coping skills are a huge part of creating healthy self-esteem.

Last year, I developed an excruciating migraine. I had never had one before or since. It lasted for days, so I eventually ended up at the doctor. He diagnosed it as a migraine and asked if I wanted pills or suppositories for the prescription.

I said, "Definitely pills." He asked if I was married. "Yes, why?" I asked.

He explained that suppositories worked better but needed to be inserted by someone else.

I told him I wouldn't be married much longer if I brought home suppositories. Although my husband is a fabulous dentist, that is not the cavity he is used to working on.

Let me add here that you do not have to be as wacky and daring as my family with your practical jokes. For some personality types I may have just horrified you with all my personal antics. This humor works for *my* family. What will work for *yours?* Create your own memories through your own flavor of humor and laughter. Surprise your children by stepping out of your comfort zone and being funny. They will love you for it. Besides, it throws them off guard and makes them wonder what you will do next. It is always to your advantage to keep them guessing.

Go buy your cans of Silly String®. Hide them in a bag. Next, announce in a stern, firm voice that there is a family meeting. Play your part well by remaining extremely serious. Your kids will fear you have discovered what they hoped you would never learn. There is always something you don't know about.

As you begin your solemn and fear-inducing soliloquy, quickly pull out your can and begin the damage. They will scream! They will laugh! They will grab their own can and get you back! They will remember this day forever! It will be one of many to come.

Box Talks

Journal Time

1. Write about a time when you had a meltdown over something minor and found yourself laughing over it later. Could your experience have gone differently if you laughed at the moment instead of waiting?

2. Think back to your last difficult day. How did you act with your kids in the midst of the stressful circumstances? What could you have done differently?

3. Where can you lighten up and add some fun in your life? Think up a few ideas for how you can accomplish that.

Family Time

1. In addition to the Silly String® fight, create
    your own activity that enhances humor and
    fun. I once asked my children individually if
    sometime as a surprise I could throw a pie in
    their face. They each said I could if they could
    do the same. We agreed it would occur only
    outside. When it finally happened, we were
    laughing so hard and had so much fun. We
    never enjoyed dessert more! If pie fights scare
    you, wear a rain poncho. They cost about a dol-
    lar and are disposable. You can set the rules as
    to what you are comfortable with. The main
    rule is to have fun!

2. When I see a family for therapy, it is a require-
    ment, not a suggestion, that the family has
    a daily positive interaction time. It sounds
    very clinical but it is very easy and extremely
    rewarding. It works like this. Every family
    member must go around and say 2 positive
    things to each member of the family. Meal time
    is usually a good time, but do what works best
    for your individual family. If you are the mom
    in the family, you will say 2 complimentary
    self-esteeming boosting comments to each
    child, stepchild and parent at the table. I've had
    children as young as 2 years old be able to par-
    ticipate. Try to be more creative than saying,
    "Nice hair and nice shirt!" Look for qualities

unique to that person. Look for opportunities where a member showed kindness, generosity and unselfishness. Believe it or not, it is fun to do this. You'll end up laughing and feeling more confident. Oh and by the way if someone slips in a negative comment like, "Your room looks very nice today, although it was looking like the city garbage dump!" then that person must share 2 extra positives.

3. Pin the Tail on the Donkey: If you are old enough you remember this childhood party game. I myself never found it that amusing. I like my version better. Blindfold the member of your family with the best sense of humor. This selection process is the most critical in determining the success of this activity. After the family member is blindfolded, you tell them you are bringing in a donkey. No! You are not going to bring in a real donkey. Just because I've done some bizarre pranks in my lifetime does not mean I'm bringing livestock in my living room. It is an exercise in imagination. Then ask them to point to various parts of the invented animal. Point to the donkey's ear. Point to the donkey's stomach. Point to the donkey's back. Then when this activity is really looking lame and boring, you ask them to point to the donkey's tail. At that precise

moment, you stick a full jar of chunky peanut butter into their hand as far up as you can thrust it. You can see why this is a lot more fun than the original version. Now you know why you are to choose the family member with the best sense of humor. You may also want to pick the slowest runner!

CHAPTER 7

Bubbles

"A smile starts on the lips. A grin spreads
to the eyes. A chuckle comes from the
belly; but a good laugh bursts from the
soul, overflows and bubbles all around."

— CAROLYN BIRMINGHAM

I N MY EARLY 20's I worked at the county hospital in
the emergency room at John Peter Smith. I worked
in the Crisis Stabilization Unit and saw patients with
emotional issues. No day was ever the same. When the
moon was full, so was the ER, full to the brink with
every mentally ill person in Tarrant County, Texas.

One afternoon, two paramedics approached
me stating they had just delivered the most unsta-
ble patient they had ever seen, explaining he was

Parenting Out of the Box

extremely dangerous and even they were scared of him. Obviously I asked, "What's wrong with him?"

"He thinks he's invisible," they responded. "Be careful, Pam. He's in Trauma Room 3."

I had seen a lot in my short time working at the hospital, but I have to confess they had me pretty concerned as I slowly approached Trauma Room 3. I timidly opened the curtains, as I stealthily stepped into the room. I look around, and there is nobody in there. No one.

For a second I thought, "Oh my gosh! He really *is* invisible."

I then turned back around to find an emergency room full of doctors, nurses, technicians, and those two paramedics now laughing so hard I think they are going to need to be admitted themselves.

They finally got me!

The next novelty toy we pull out of the box is a bottle of bubbles equipped with a plastic wand to make it all happen. Stick it in, pull out the wand and blow colored, iridescent bubbles all over the back yard. Blow a magical stream of beautiful rainbow bubbles over in delight then someone comes along with a big, straight pin to pop them one by one.

I wanted to be a counselor since I was very young. When I finally decided to major in Psychology after walking away from my Theatre scholarship, no one supported my idea. People at church feared the classes

114

would lead me to be an atheist or worse. My mother even invited over several women to our house who had allegedly achieved PhDs so she could "prove" you rarely get what you want out of such a degree. Amazingly, all those "educated women" held jobs at fast food chains, shoe stores or the sanitation department.

Undeterred, I still felt God wanted me to pursue counseling, even though not one single person in my life was supportive about Psychology. I am telling you, my bubble was burst so many times I don't know how I followed through with my dream. But God had a plan for me to be in counseling none the less, so here I am, despite the discouragement and frustration.

❖   ❖   ❖

Bubbles

What bubbles are you bursting of your child's dreams, hopes, and wishes?

> *Child:* "Mommy, I want to make movies and be able to have them shown in theatres when I have a job!"

> *Mom:* (as she is bursting the bubble) "Do you know how unlikely that is to ever happen? You are no Steven Spielberg! There are people all over Hollywood a whole lot more talented than you who are waiting tables at restaurants and sleeping in cars. (bursting

the remaining bubbles) Goodness, think of something sensible!"

Child: "Dad when I grow up I really want to be a fireman! I want to save people and rescue animals. It will be so much fun to drive a fire truck."

Dad: (seeing the bubbles floating all around and piercing each one with a sharp pop) "I hope you are kidding! That is way too dangerous! I am not having my son be a firefighter. Do you want to give your mother a heart attack? She would be worried sick about you every day. Find a job where you can make some money."

Every time another bubble bursts, they feel a little more discouraged and defeated. When a child feels his ideas are not good enough, he then concludes that *he* is just not good enough. This is a crucial point in the development of self-esteem and self-confidence. Sadly, many parents have a bigger bubble-popping pin than an attentive listening ear.

Undivided Attention
Parents, it is vital to practice good listening skills when your child or stepchild is attempting to discuss anything with you. Love your child enough to stop what you are doing and maintain eye contact while she is speaking. With technology and smart phone addictions

these days, one-on-one in person communication is too often rudely interrupted by calls, texts and alerts, as though the person in front of you is not important. Undivided attention is a gift so seldom given when it is gift so desperately needed.

Act as though you are interested in what your child is saying, even if you are not. You do it with strangers at the grocery store, at the office or at the bank. You can handle doing it with your children. If not, one day your teenager may not want to talk to you anymore. You won't know when that day will arrive. It just will. Prevent that heartbreak by treating every conversation as though it matters to you because it matters to your child. Treat it as the treasure it is. You won't be perfect at this I know, but determine to make the effort.

In counseling sessions I have passed on vast wisdom to my clients. This includes the importance of two extremely valuable words utilized in the exchange of information. Research (my own) indicates that by using these time-proven terms you can ensure successful communication. These words are very complicated so prepare yourself by sitting down and taking a deep breath. Get your pencils out. Ready? Here we go.

The words are "Really" and "Wow".

You are now realizing this book is much deeper than originally thought. When my children come home with the stories of their day, I'm listening. All I am saying is, "Really" and "Wow" so they feel like I'm connected, interested and involved in what they are communicating. Kids and adults alike just want to know that someone cares enough to listen to their story. That is all anyone wants. You don't want advice. You don't want suggestions. You just want to talk without interruption. You want your bubble admired and enjoyed, not punctured and popped.

Dream a Little Dream

When your children share their dreams and aspirations with you, don't burst their bubble. We all need to have dreams. Whether the dreams are unrealistic or impractical doesn't matter when you're in elementary school. Many of my teenaged clients have shared with me that the number one problem they have with their parents or stepparents is that they don't listen to them. Teens feel lectured, advised, counseled, and suggested to, but rarely listened to.

Let them think their dreams matter. Let them dream a little to you. Give your child permission to be creative and inventive. It is fun to pretend you might be famous one day. As a parent you must believe in the dream. It is imperative that you believe he can do anything that Gods leads him to do.

Proverbs 22:6 tells us, "Train up a child in the way he should go, and when he is old he will not depart from it." The passage clearly does not say train up a child the way you want him to be. Clearly, becoming a rock star may never happen. It is still adventuresome to consider it as a possibility. You might be thinking, "Well, if I act like I'm encouraging something crazy like that he just might do it!" Remember how many times you changed what you were going to be when you grew up or how many times you changed your major in college? That's part of growing up.

Affirming Dreams

Besides, if you always discourage your kids hopes and wishes for their life, they will do everything in their power to prove you wrong. Children need their dreams affirmed because that affirms them as a person. Building self-confidence occurs as you permit your child to visualize their possible potential. Often kids are just expressing creative ideas that are fun to think about. They are not necessarily filling out their degree plan for college.

In a blended family, sometimes a child will feel like their stepparent automatically rejects any creative or different opinion or outlook. When you became a stepparent, you became that child's 3rd or 4th parent. You signed up for this. You probably didn't know how challenging it would be, but here you are. Your responsibilities include enhancing and building self-esteem in your stepchild's life. It is an awesome privilege and honor.

Philippians 2:14-15 is a wonderful scripture for parents and children alike to memorize and ponder frequently: "Do all things without grumbling or disputing, that you may be blameless and innocent, children of God without blemish in the midst of a crooked and twisted generation, among whom you shine as lights in the world." Parents shining as lights in the world point their children toward shining the same.

The next time your child or stepchild shares their dreams and hopes, be supportive and encouraging. Remember these words: "Really!" "Wow!" You don't have to agree with their idea or concept. They aren't asking for your opinion or advice anyway. So if your child doesn't ask for your advice, don't give it. She won't listen anyway. Be confident that you've raised her well. She will ask for your opinion when she needs it. Often she doesn't want your input. She just wants you to watch her blow her beautiful bubbles, listen and dream along. The next time your child communicates creative, innovative thoughts or dreams, do not burst their bubble. Let them float and bounce around the room.

Box Talks

Journal Time

1. What bubble was burst early in your life? Write about it. If it was a dream to pursue singing, painting or other creative art, check out taking a class in it now. It's not too late to enjoy a hobby of a long lost dream.

2. Write out all your dreams you can remember from your childhood. Did your dreams change? Did you give up? Or what? And what about schooling? Did you change majors in college more than once?

3. For an entire day notice how you interact with your kids. Are you looking them in the eye and ignoring technology when they are telling you a story? Write about what you discover then write what areas you need to work on.

Family Time

1. Go blow bubbles outside. Get the ones with a big wand and chase them in the backyard. It is fun for all ages.

2. Have each member talk about their fantasy dream job, not the one that is practical, the one that is fun.

3. Have each member tell a funny story or joke to the family.

CHAPTER 8

Pom Poms

"Instruction does much, but
encouragement everything."

— JOHANN WOLFGANG VON GOETHE

AM SITTING IN MY OFFICE finishing up a session when
I hear all this commotion in the waiting room. I hear
screaming and cussing, then a lamp crashing to the
floor. Sorry, session over. I open my door to find my
next appointment—The entire family is agitated and
upset, not to mention my lamp is shattered.

The parents begin to share how they had just left
the mall. Their 10-year-old son wanted an expensive
toy, above their budget. He was not going to take
"No" for an answer. They said he had thrown himself

down on the floor and began to throw a tantrum in the middle of the store.

He admitted to me that he had been kicking, screaming, and yelling that he better get that toy or he wasn't leaving the store. So I asked the obvious question of the parents.

"What did you do?"

And the answer should astound you.

They bought him the toy.

The parents said their son refused to leave unless they bought him that toy. They had to get to this appointment so they just bought it so they could leave. Why were they fighting in the waiting room? The parents didn't want me to know about the toy so they were demanding it stay in the car. For some reason, they thought I might not agree with their choice to purchase it.

I never told them that I disagreed. I did tell them that if they didn't take the toy back they would never resolve their problems. The parents needed to take a firm stand if they were ever going to get control returned to them. To their credit, they returned the toy, took control back from the 10-year-old, and began a new life for the whole family.

❖ ❖ ❖

Pom Poms

The next toy in the box is Pom Poms. Where do you find them? You find them in the hands of cheerleaders of course. Pom Poms are imperative for developing healthy self-esteem and confidence in any child. Pick up those Pom Poms, shake them wildly and cheer your child on to victory. It may sound corny but truly, children crave love, attention and praise. Children desperately need to be noticed and acknowledged as they make positive decisions. I Thessalonians 5:11 blesses us with, "Therefore encourage one another and build one another up, just as you are doing."

Cheering your child on towards success often means making difficult choices. It is hard to say "No" when you want to please your child. It is embarrassing to have your 10-year-old throwing a public tantrum. It is always easier to be a bad parent and give in rather than a good parent and hold firm with "No." A good parent is their child's cheerleader indeed, but a cheerleader who cheers on good behavior and steers him away from bad. Even a cheerleader has to determine when to make critical moves.

Sadly, many parents believe children should not be praised for exhibiting minimal requirements of behavior. A large number of parents feel positive reinforcement should not be utilized for basic rules of behavior. It is expected for children to follow the rules. They shouldn't need a pep rally as a reward for just doing the essentials. I disagree with those parents and have over thirty years of counseling children to back up this view point as well as scripture. I Thessalonians 4:18 says, "Therefore encourage one another with these words."

It is extremely important to provide children with positive reinforcement. You can never do it enough. Children need it almost as much as food and water. With all of the problems children and adolescents face today, it should be acknowledged when they make positive choices. If you are blessed to have children who are responsible and make good decisions, they deserve to be complimented daily for it. If the opposite were true, believe me, you would be focusing on their daily deficits or problems.

In her bestselling book *Supernanny*, author Jo Frost puts it best. "Positive attention and praise are the most effective rewards for children. They are immediate, and reinforce good behavior on the spot."[12]

If you do not have the good fortune to be rearing the perfect child, which is all of us, then you will have to be more creative. Continually search for ways you can encourage, exhort, and build up your child. Constantly be aware of ways you can bless your child with words of affirmation. Look for opportunities where you can praise her for how she handled a certain situation.

The Opportunity

There was a young man who was looking for an opportunity. He needed a job. He had recently moved to California and was interviewing at a large department store. This store had literally any item you could ever want to purchase.

The manager of the store really liked the young man. Although the applicant had no sales experience, the manager decided to give him the job. At the end of the young man's first day of work, the manager came down to see how he fared.

Manager: "So, how did the first day go?"

Salesman: "It went pretty well I think."

Manager: "How many sales did you make?"

Salesman: "One."

Manager: "One! My goodness, most sales people make between 40–50 sales! How much was the sale for?"

Salesman: "$164,872.00."

Manager: $164,872.00! What did you sell?"

Salesman: "Well, first a man was wandering through the Fishing Department. So I asked him what kind of lure he liked to fish with. Then I asked him if he needed a new fishing rod, which he did. Next he told me he really liked deep sea fishing so I walked him over to the Boating Department. The customer then realized that his Honda Civic would not be able to pull such a large boat, so we went to the Automotive Department where I sold him a 4x4 Blazer."

> Manager: "A man comes in to buy a fishing lure, and you sell him a boat and truck?"
>
> Salesman: "No, actually he came in to buy his wife a box of tampons. I told him, 'Your weekend is shot. You might as well go fishing!'"

That young salesman found an opportunity and clearly mastered the art of encouragement. You too have daily opportunities you can seize to encourage your children that will deliver results far more lasting than this one day sale. Begin elevating his self-confidence today and you will train him up to be a self-assured, healthy adult.

Other than providing spiritual guidance, building self-esteem is one of the most important things you can do as a parent or stepparent. The long-term effects will outlive you. This is one of the legacies and inheritances you are leaving your children. How a child is encouraged and built up dramatically impacts his self-worth. And building confidence affects a child's choices, decisions, and even values in virtually every area of their life. Self-esteem affects an individual throughout a lifetime. An insecure person can easily be spotted within the first five minutes of meeting. Insecurity directly corresponds to low self-esteem.

Insecurity will not get you a promotion at work. It will not assist in getting better grades or making more friends. Instead, insecurity leads to friction, frustration, and failure. As parents, you have tremendous influence to build security and confidence in your children. It is not too late. Begin by demonstrating emotional support, regardless of circumstances. Children need to feel loved and encouraged even when there is disobedience. The child should always feel unconditional love even if he is grounded for a year.

Consequences are Inevitable

Consequences are part of developing healthy individuals. Sadly, some parents are misguided into believing that they "love their child too much" to hand down a consequence. This is the absolute worst thing you could ever do to your child. Eventually there will be consequences by someone else, if not by you—be it a teacher, employer or police officer. A child with no experience of boundaries will grow up to be spoiled and self-absorbed. Oh woe to the individual who marries your darling or hires her for employment.

Parents who feel guilty about allowing their children to experience natural consequences are typically insecure themselves and overly worried about being "liked" by their kids rather than respected. If emphasis is on being popular with your children so they won't be angry with you, then you may be a great friend but an ineffective parent. Eventually every single person faces consequences in life, both positive and negative. Rescuing children from negative consequences leaves them unprepared for the realities of life that Mom and Dad can't fix.

Yes, this is still the Pom Poms chapter where encouragement and praise are the focal point. As parents, it is critical to encourage, not enable. Often there is a fine line between the two.

Enabling actually harms your child and delays emotional growth. An enabling parent may feel like she is helping and encouraging, but the reality is quite different. Enabling is often encouraging a child to continue with poor decisions and unacceptable behavior. Responsible parenting should never include supporting irresponsible behavior.

Encourage your child for their *character.* Look for opportunities when your child reaches out to help around the house, even in small ways. In doing family therapy for over 30 years, I have found that most families do not express appreciation to each other. Family members may think positive things about each other but rarely express it out loud to one another. Nobody seems to have a problem expressing feelings about the negative, less favorable behavior, however.

Appreciate and Express

Think about all the blessings that you have with your child. There are many qualities that you appreciate but probably don't comment on. You appreciate his willingness to go to school without complaining. You appreciate the completion of chores. You appreciate your child who is the peacemaker when other siblings "stir it up." You appreciate his positive attitude at church and then there are 100 more great qualities you can think of.

Make a commitment that anytime a positive thought comes to mind about another human being, you will share it from this day forward. It is a wonderful feeling to bless your child, your spouse, and your friends with encouraging words. Remember the last time you were paid a compliment? That good feeling lasted all day long. What a privilege to bless your family with good memories that last forever. Personally, I'd like to be remembered as the cheerleader mom, not the screaming one. Regretfully, I have at times played both parts well.

Even if you don't like a certain football team, you still like the cheerleaders. Everyone loves the cheerleaders even if they are on a team that you hate. They are positive, upbeat, energetic, happy, bubbly, and entertaining. I have been a cheerleader in every school I attended until college. Then I majored in Psychology and really learned how to become a true cheerleader. I am never happier than when I am cheering my kids to another victory or consoling them after a defeat. You don't have to wear the uniform to share the spirit of encouragement. (Thank goodness I don't have to wear the uniform today!)

Even after an agonizing defeat, the cheerleaders are still there, still encouraging, "It's okay! Get them in the next game!" There will always be another game and another opportunity to build up and exhort your player.

Box Talks

Journal Time

1. Ponder the character of each of your children. Write down a positive description of your child's traits then find opportunities to compliment them.

2. What contributions to the household can you genuinely compliment your kids for? Think about all the things mentioned in this chapter of what you can compliment. Notice these about your kids and begin to verbalize your appreciation.

3. Write down the last compliment you were paid. Who made the compliment? How did you feel? Who in your life is consistent with complimenting you? Thank them today for being a cheerleader in your life.

Family Time

1. As a family watch a funny movie together. Some of my old favorites are *Ferris Bueller's Day Off, What About Bob?, Elf,* and *National Lampoon's Vacation.* Oldies but goodies. Make popcorn and buy candy.

2. Play video games with your kids, and don't be a sore loser when they beat you.

3. Volunteer at a local shelter, and serve food to the homeless. It is the best activity you'll share as a family.

CHAPTER 9
The Train

"Train up a child in the way that he should go
and when he is old, he will not depart from it."

— KING SOLOMON

A CLIENT CAME IN, like so many other parents,
starting out by telling me that before she gave
me all the details, she wanted me to know that she
was not going to violate her son's privacy by going
through his belongings, but she desperately needed
advice on what to do otherwise. She feared for her
teenage son's welfare, but felt it was too invasive to
look through his room.

"If your child was kidnapped and you had no
idea who did it, would you feel guilty going through
his things for clues then?"

"Of course I wouldn't in that dire situation," she agreed.

I assured her that she was just as desperate to find clues and evidence now. He was a minor. She was his parent, his guardian. His welfare was her responsibility, and her son was in the midst of a major crisis. She took my advice and went through his room, cell phone and computer while he was not home. She found he had been "kidnapped" by drugs, and alcohol. He had raped a girl and was suicidal. If she hadn't investigated his room, he might not be here today. His mother saved his life by loving him enough to investigate his belongings. The next day, he actually took a train to a treatment facility and worked hard to put his life together.

❖　❖　❖

Train

Get ready to board because the next toy in the box is a train. The train provides security and rest. I have enjoyed riding the train at Six Flags Over Texas since I was a child. The train offered rest from walking. You could also view the entire park during the ride. From the view of that particular train, you could see where you wanted to go next and which ride looked the most exciting. The train provided perspective. Often as parents, you need to sit back, rest a little and try to determine where you want to go next. Take all the time you need. The conductor lets you ride as long as you want.

At an amusement park, it might seem more fun, more exciting, and more thrilling to ride a roller coaster. The lines are usually longer for the roller coaster and the squeals are always louder. Staying on the roller coaster for too long, however, could prove to be dangerous and may even make you sick. If you are pregnant or have heart problems, you are not even supposed to get on one because of the potential threat to your health. The train, however, gets you where you want to go through continuous, progressive and diligent effort.

Teenagers Emotions are Like Roller Coasters

Let's take a look at the lives of teenagers for a moment. Their emotions are much like riding a roller coaster— up and down, happy one moment and then miserable the next, quickly sliding downward into anger or depression.

Remember what it was like to be a teenager? It was hard. As teens, we always wanted to grow up and we couldn't wait to be out on our own. As teens, we wanted to test our own wings to see if we could fly. We used to be teenagers. Remember that ride? Remember how hard it was? Things were changing all the time.

Here is a key thing to remember as we parent our own teens: Take time to remember as best you can what it was like to be that age. And words to the wise—don't start the 'Back in my day we had to walk five miles to school and all of it uphill...' stories. Remember so you can reflect how they feel in order to connect with your children. If you start telling stories of your youth, chances are your teen will simply tune you out. It is really important to reflect back to when you were the age of your kids you are trying to train. The more you can understand what it is like for him, the better chance you have of relating. Not necessarily to say, "Back in my day," because they won't really care. It is more about feeling your own connection to them.

The emotional roller coaster young people board is unpredictable and uncertain. Their pressures and issues today are extremely stressful as they often face unplanned curves and descents. So it is often safer to get on the train or so it would seem. As I was writing the chapter I noticed *The Fort Worth Star Telegram's* headline one day said: "Derailed Train was hauling Hazardous Cargo."[13] How true for our youth. If they are putting unhealthy material into their bodies and minds, they will derail.

Don't Accept "The Phase"
Parents today are far too accepting of their offspring's inappropriate behavior. Teens are inviting drugs, alcohol, tobacco, pornography and sex into their existence. Sadly, many parents dismiss these behaviors as a "typical teenage phase." For some, "the phase" becomes a way of life. As a parent, you may be holding the dice to your teen's future. Roll the dice and the outcome could be getting your kids help. It could also be rolling the dice and letting them do anything

they want as long as it makes them happy. Which do you think has the better chance?

Your children get to practice life at your house until they cement life in their own. Don't permit any harmful behavior, not at any level. As you know, anything you practice long enough becomes a habit, and the more you do it, the more perfected that skill becomes (wanted or unwanted). Some parents tend to be naïve about what is actually going on with their children. You don't want to imagine the worst, so you don't even consider the possibilities.

Drug and alcohol use is at an all time high. I have more children, teenagers, and adults in my office for substance abuse than ever. Most of the young people I treat in therapy don't see smoking pot as a problem, even though it may have cost them a job, their education, or even a place to live. I have also seen middle-aged marijuana users who still live with their senior citizen parents who once maintained the same philosophy.

The problem with doing any kind of drugs is that one cannot predict who will develop lifelong issues and become an addict. Too many parents have regretfully ignored their children's negative choices for fear of alienating them. You are only delaying what you eventually will be forced to deal with. The price is literally exponentially higher to dealing with it later, and the success rate of breaking addiction equally less.

While your child is a minor, you have more options for intervention than when she becomes an adult. Don't be afraid to take a firm stand. Tough love is called tough for a reason. It is difficult to be strong when you really feel like caving, especially when you feel guilty. If your child is making bad choices, why should you feel guilty about trying to save her life?

Junior Executive Training

You want to train Junior to be successful. You want to train him to make quality and positive decisions. You certainly don't want to train Junior to become more proficient at reckless behavior, and yet if you ignore his bad choice, that's exactly what you are doing. Again, parents who have knowledge of their child's problems and do nothing to save their child must understand the high price they will be paying. At some point, you can't look the other way because the issue is surrounding everywhere you look.

Sexual addiction, sexual abuse, pornography, drunk driving, texting nude pictures or sexting, selling, buying, and using drugs, have all been issues brought into my office on a regular basis. And they are usually followed up by those clients' younger siblings doing the same. Usually, the parents know about it already. You may be appalled, but sometimes well-meaning parents just don't know what to do. They hope it will go away before there is a real problem. Here's your wake up call—the *first time* is when you have a real problem!

Deliver grace and love to your children, yes, but in doing so include zero tolerance for unacceptable behavior. What kids do as children and teenagers prepares them for what to do in adulthood. As author Andy Andrews says: "It is exponentially more difficult to find employment for a 25-year-old with bad manners than for a 25-year-old with good manners."[14] And the one with bad manners will be unemployed over and over and growing more bitter and clueless as to why everyone is out to get him. Much of the marriage counseling I perform is due to poor childhood behavior spilling into adulthood because parents refused to deal with it. When you repeat a behavior long enough you get real good at it. Practice makes perfect, right? More like a perfect disaster following every aspect of life.

In *Have a New Kid by Friday,* Kevin Leman writes, "As a result today's kids are growing more and more powerful. They're all about 'me, me, me' and 'gimme.' They are held accountable less and have fewer responsibilities in the family. To them, family is about not what you can give but what you can get. Fewer children today consider others before themselves because they've never been taught to think that way."[15]

My mother wrote a high school paper on juvenile delinquency. Her conclusion boldly ended with, "Stop juvenile delinquency in the high chair, not the electric chair." Her message then is the same as mine today. The sooner you deal with a problem, the better chances you have of a favorable outcome. You *will* deal with the problem eventually. The longer the wait, the bigger and stronger the demon becomes.

There are only a few precious years that you have been privileged to train up your children. Use every moment wisely. Be inquisitive. Look for clues and information about their life. Search their room, their computer, their phone, their journal, their backpack, and their car. You are not invading their private space. You are their guardian, their protector, and their advisor. Parents also need to become the private investigator at home. You need all the knowledge you can ascertain.

Proverbs 5:13 states, "I have not obeyed the voice of my teachers nor submitted and consented to those who instructed me."

The following box is a tool for parents to spark ideas in ways to discover as much about your child's behavior as possible. Many parents struggle with guilt about sneaking around and going through their child's belongings. You are not doing this to be invasive. You are searching for information to ensure that your child or teen is not in trouble. Get over feeling guilty. You just might come across something that could save him from a dangerous situation. That is your only motivation. Often times teens will not volunteer that they are experiencing a crisis. Many kids have actually been relieved when their parents "found out" because hiding secrets is extremely stressful. Sometimes kids want help but don't know how to ask for it. They are afraid of getting in trouble when all you want to do is provide aid. If you found marijuana in your son's room, your primary focus would be getting him help, not necessarily going straight to consequences.

Here are some tips to catch your perpetuator so you can SNOOP:

S – Surveillance. *Read their emails, texts, journals, diaries, Facebook, Twitter and phones. In surveying their Facebook account you also learn valuable information about their friends. Look in their drawers, books, backpacks, and cars. Search any place that you would hide something, like the vent in their bedroom. Do you feel guilty about doing this? Not unless their name is on the mortgage of your home.*

N – Notice. *Take notice of anything out of the ordinary. Any changes in how they dress, act, or speak. Are their eating and sleeping habits different? Track their financial spending. Notice changes with friends, like dropping friends or gaining new friends.*

O – Opinion. *Is your child's opinion about issues changing? Did he used to enjoy church and now doesn't see the need for it. Is his opinion about drinking and drugs changing? Are there changes in his opinion on social issues?*

O – Obedience. *Is your child disobeying the rules? Is she lying? Is she coming home later than her curfew? Is she disrespectful when speaking with you? Is she not doing as well in school?*

P – Persevere and Pray. *Keep on checking up on your child, not because you are paranoid but because it is your responsibility. You let the kids know that you may occasionally check their things to encourage quality decisions. When you do check, it is unnecessary to announce it. Do it when they are not around. Pray continually when they are and aren't around.*

The more information you have, the better decisions you can make for your children. Here are just a few of the issues parents have discovered by taking an active role in learning as much as possible about their child:

1. Child was being bullied at school

2. Teenager had been shoplifting

3. Found empty liquor bottles

4. Brother was sexually molesting younger sibling

5. Stepfather was molesting stepchild

6. Found evidence that teen was a drug dealer

7. Internet pornography addiction

8. Sexually explicit pictures sent from phone and computer

9. Found heroin

10. Child had plan to commit suicide

11. Unpaid traffic citations and warrants

And there are so many more. The more information you possess, the better equipped you are to deal with any adversity your child is facing. Sticking your head in the sand is never a wise parenting skill. You can't determine if your child is on the right track if you don't even know what direction he is headed.

You may think everything is fine, but that light at the end of the tunnel may be an oncoming train instead!

All Aboard

Several years ago, my husband and I took an Amtrak train from Fort Worth, Texas to Chicago. It was wonderful. We had never taken a 24-hour train trip anywhere, so it was an adventure. The scenery was beautiful and the meals were fabulous.

The sleeping arrangements left much to be desired. When you go to sleep in your compartment at night, you're basically harnessed in with a seat belt type of restraint to the bunk bed. Without it you will go flying across the compartment during the night with all the twists, turns and stops on the train's journey. Even though a train is more stable than a roller coaster, there is still danger of sliding into the bathroom.

Train passengers, children and teens all need restraints. Children crave boundaries to feel secure. Most of the teenagers that I've counseled actually tell me that they are happier when they are grounded because they have an excuse to not make poor decisions. They have a temporary "out" from peer pressure.

Psycho Parents

It is hard to believe but true. Teens are grateful to be rescued from stressful situations, including the pressure of partying. Almost every teen I've ever seen in therapy has said that the temptation to drink alcohol, use drugs, and have sex is overwhelming. Many teens are relieved when their parents drug test them because then it becomes a convenient excuse. "I'd love to party with you but my 'psycho parents' drug test me," is a popular saying with the kids I see. They've been given an easy out from peer pressure.

The pressure on young people today is more than parents can imagine. I've had many teenagers tell me that their life would be better if they were grounded for the rest of high school. It seems as though for many teens, the moment the restriction is lifted is the moment they fall back into making unhealthy choices.

Determine what boundaries are necessary for your child to be as successful as possible. Does she need more restraint in her life because she is unable to do that for herself? Is he making better decisions now so you can ease up and give him a bit more control and freedom? Watch and learn. She will let you know by her choices and behavior if you need to intervene and adjust the game plan.

Be vigilant. Be observant. Be praying. Ask God for wisdom in how to effectively deal with your child. Ask God for wisdom in how to communicate with your child in ways that he will be receptive to. I don't have all the answers, but I have a God who does.

Let your child's toy train remind you to train him up in the way he should go to avoid a train wreck. None of us are perfect and even the most loving parents can raise children who go astray. Your goal is to help your children leave childhood with as little baggage as possible. Is he becoming the person he was destined to be, or is he stuck on the roller-coaster of poor choices with consequences? You want your precious child to get to his final destination and fulfill his destiny.

Box Talks

Journal Time

1. React to the beginning of the chapter and the mother who was afraid to check up on her son. Write out how you feel about snooping on your kids? Is this uncomfortable for you? Do you understand why it is important to keep watch on your kids?

2. What decisions have you made about your parenting for the next time your child displays inappropriate behavior?

3. Think back on your teen years. Write out what punishments worked best on you and which ones didn't.

Family Time

Go in your child's room one day with a notebook and ask if you can interview him or her. Here are your questions. Write down their answers.

1. What will you do differently as a parent than I have done?

2. How will you do it better?

3. What would you do if you found out your child was doing drugs, drinking, or having sex?

4. What would you do to make your family more fun than our family is now?

5. What do you feel is unfair?

6. How will you teach your kids to make good decisions?

7. When your child makes a mistake how will you handle it?

8. How will you get your child to open up and communicate with you?

9. What do you want to teach your children about God?

10. What will you do with your kids that we didn't do with you?

You will learn more about your child by this simple exercise. You may even get a few good ideas you can start using that day.

CHAPTER 10

The Medical Kit

"We're all like broken toys in the
repair shop; waiting for that one
person to come along and fix us."

— UNKNOWN

⁓

A SWEET, INNOCENT LITTLE GIRL entered my office. She was 7 years old and scared to talk. She didn't want to get into more trouble than she was already in. In a few moments, her father would enter the session. He admittedly had sexually molested her, not once, but many times. They were here for court-committed counseling. If they missed their appointment, he went to jail.

When their session was over, in came the next little girl with basically the same gut- wrenching story.

Parenting Out of the Box

Those were the only type of appointments I had all day long, all week long, all month long, all semester long. Welcome to my first graduate internship. I was treating fathers who didn't really think they did anything wrong. Their only motivation to show up for counseling was to avoid incarceration.

During those sessions, I cried everyday going to and from work. Many times, I literally threw up after a session. Being in the presence of unrepentant evil was the most horrible thing I have ever faced. I wanted to save all those little girls and take them away to somewhere safe. No one protected them, not their parents, not the system, not even me. I couldn't do anything more.

People ask me all the time, "How do you listen to people's problems all day long? Doesn't it wear you out?" Thankfully, God has blessed me with much better coping skills than I had when I started my counseling career. To this day, however, the cases that always haunt me, are those ones where precious children have been sexually abused by someone they trust.

In *The Power of a Positive Teen*, authors Karol, Grace, and Joy Ladd write, "Just because our circumstances are difficult doesn't mean that God has left us. Actually, these are the times we can stand back and see the hand of God at work all the more, helping us to make it through. God doesn't promise that our lives will go smoothly; he promises that he will be with us in the midst of our struggles. He will never leave us."[16]

The pain in your life that needs to be repaired may not be from sexual abuse. But everyone has been hurt by someone. We are all imperfect humans, and everybody hurts sometimes.

There is only One who can repair our brokenness, and that is God. Being that He made you in the first place, it would seem He would have the schematics and warranty information on file.

Praying Everyday

Too many Christians treat God like characters do in daytime dramas or soap operas. The soap stars pray when someone goes in the hospital and not for any other reason or at any other time. Here's some insight: Perhaps it would make for a less dramatic life if you developed the habit of praying over your kids before the chaos appeared. God is always there, even if you don't want Him, and even if you don't believe in Him. He's just waiting for you to call on Him.

If you could really change yourself and your circumstances, why haven't you already done it? You can't do it on your own. We all need help from a source bigger than ourselves. Begin praying instead of worrying, and your life will change.

For decades, I have encouraged parents to pray over their sleeping children and teens. Pray positive words of affirmation and you will see answers to your prayers.

❖　❖　❖

The Medical Kit

The final toy in the box is the beloved medical kit ready to repair real and imaginary scars and wounds. My own medical kit was my personal favorite toy throughout elementary school. I carried it everywhere. I loved to refill the bandages and dressing, constantly attempting to repair everything and everyone with something from my kit.

What a happy day when someone scraped their knee or got a splinter! It probably was for the best that I never actually entered the medical field, but back then, I was the neighborhood medic. It was very rewarding for me to see people get better. It still is. But as I grew older, I found those toy medical tools were metaphors for bigger issues of life. My medical kit had it all—stethoscope to check for the beating heart, otoscope for the ears and eyes, blood pressure monitor to check out the stress and mess, tongue depressor for the throat and tonsils, thermometer for the fever, gauze & bandages for the wounds and ointment to soothe the pain.

The Stethoscope

In my old medical kit, there was a stethoscope where I would listen to a beating heart. The heart was always healthy in my examinations but not always true in reality. I recommend listening to the heart of your child. Some of you believe he no longer has one, but if he is breathing, he does.

The Otoscope for Ears and Eyes

Listen to hear what is really happening with your child. Often what comes out of the mouth is not what is in his heart. You think he isn't trying if he is doing poorly in school. Then you discover he is being bullied and feeling suicidal. If you know something is wrong, but don't know what, counseling is always an option.

Often counseling can uncover hidden truths that need to be exposed. You can't deal with a problem if you don't even know there is one. If your assumption ends up being wrong, the worst that can happen is that you've spent a few dollars and you feel relieved.

The otoscope is also for looking into the ears. You may be wondering if your teen can actually hear you anymore. She never seems to listen to a single word you say. Don't forget to use that same instrument on the eyes. After all, she used to think you were a genius, but now she just rolls her eyes when you utter brilliant dialogue. Be sure and examine the eyes next with that same otoscope to see what is up with the rolling of the eyes you've been spotting when she walks past you.

The Tongue Depressor

One of the most helpful instruments in the medical kits is the tongue depressor. If only it worked better. Think how useful it would be if every time your child or teen said something obnoxious, you could stop him from speaking. Doubt it would work very well though as children's speech often mimics the parents.

I have been in the Gifted and Talented Program for the Sarcastic. I actually excelled so quickly that I began teaching the class. When my grown son was three years old, we went furniture shopping. It was not at the top of his list of fun things to do. Oddly enough, he wanted to go to a toy store.

We walked in a furniture store and a nice lady approached us saying, "Hi, you look like you're having a nice day today." My son puts both his hands on his hips and loudly proclaims, "Yeah, this is really what I want to be doing on my day off, loads of fun!" And he sounded exactly like me! That is when I dropped out of the Gifted and Talented Program. I didn't like the thought of rearing smart-mouthed sarcastic offspring. One for the whole family is one too many.

So we are back to role modeling again. Ever feel as though you are too old and too tired to model? That runway is always open. Whether you want to be there or not, you are the featured supermodel on the runway of your children's life.

The Blood Pressure Monitor

When building self-esteem in your child it is imperative to recognize when her life pressures become too great. The blood pressure cuff in a medical kit is for measuring accurate pressure. Being observant to your child's pressures will be helpful in determining how well he is coping. A child who feels overwhelmed may begin to experience anxiety and even depression. Teaching appropriate coping skills for dealing with stress will not only enhance a child's self-worth, but can prevent depression and even thoughts of suicide.

Learning how to maneuver through adversity is a lifelong skill that not only builds self-esteem, but also character. A child who feels stable and safe during times of pressure and stress is what every parent desires for each of their children.

The Thermometer

It is very rare for the patient's temperature to always be 98.6 degrees, which must mean we are not normal very often. Parents are always looking for ways to read how their kids are doing. You look for clues such as body language, facial expressions, mood, attitude and even vocal tone. Learning to read your child is similar to reading a thermometer, an item critical in the kit. It is always good practice to assess the temperature of your child's situation.

In *Everybody's Normal Till You Get To Know Them*, bestselling author John Ortberg writes, "We all want to look normal, but the writers of Scripture insist that no one is 'totally normal'—at least not as God defines normal. 'All we like sheep have gone astray,' they tell us. 'All have sinned and fall short of the glory of God.'"[17]

Some kids are great communicators and let you know anytime something is wrong or when they are feeling badly. Many are not as skilled or open. Sometimes you have to sneak up on your children and cram the thermometer in their mouth, threatening the other type of thermometer if they don't cooperate.

How can you help your kids recover if you never know something needs repairing?

Gauze and Bandages

The absolute most frequent items used in the beloved medical kit are the gauzes and bandages to cover up wounds and help everyone feel better. When you know your child has had a traumatic event, of course you want to be right there grabbing gauze and bandages to help repair the wounds, visible or invisible. Your primary focus is to get immediate help so the healing process can begin.

The Ointment

The pain relieving ointment is to soothe the pain of injury. Injuries always come with pain, so it is always merciful to rush in pain relief, be it Bactine, Neosporine or Hydrogen Peroxide. The whole purpose of the beloved medical kit is to rush in with as much assistance as possible to bring a patient back to health with as little pain and scarring as possible. Inevitably, life involves injuries—emotional and physical. You cannot grow up without getting hurt. God has placed these precious babies in your arms for eighteen years to guide them toward a life of relationship with Him. He desires for each of us to make a contribution to the world. Parents hold the "medical kit" to treat and mend their kids through the years of growing up. The most powerful pain relieving ointment a parent can find in rearing children is the power of the spoken word. Parents may never realize the magnitude and power of every spoken word, be it a simple comment or deliberate lesson. Kids are always listening even when we think they are not.

> *"A soft answer turns away wrath, but*
> *a harsh word stirs up anger."*
> — PROVERBS 15:1 ESV

Parents have many opportunities to de-escalate potential conflicts. Mothers and fathers, stepparents, and grandparents carry tremendous influence to motivate children toward excellence, even, or especially, in the moment of crisis. The power of healing words to a hurting child is limitless. Words from a respected parent can give a child the incentive to continue on when quitting seems imminent. Proverbs 12:18 holds tremendous insight. "There is one whose rash words are like sword thrusts, but the tongue of the wise brings healing."

One of my favorite scriptures in the Bible is Proverbs 18:21 and it says, "Death and life are in the power of the tongue, and those who love it will eat its fruits." Death and life? It would seem that our words are extremely important.

Prying God's Fingers

In the heat of conflict, our words will bring life or death. The decision will be totally yours. At times, I have found my mouth to be rather rebellious during times of war. Often I pray for God to shut it with his mighty hands. Then I desperately take both my hands and try to pry His fingers apart to get the last word in… this is not something I recommend.

Such is the case of a little girl I knew many years ago. There was a child who desperately needed counseling. She was in 6th grade when her world came crashing down. With absolutely no warning, her parents announced they were getting a divorce. The last night her father spent at home was filled with hysterics of pleading and crying. She remembered begging her father not to leave.

"Please Daddy, please don't move out. Please stay with us. We need you. I'll be so scared without you. Please," she cried, as she held down his legs hoping he couldn't walk away.

"Honey," he sadly replied, "I love you. I'd do anything for you, but I can't give her up. I just can't."

Her father was leaving the family for another woman. On that last evening, the little girl stood uncontrollably screaming and sobbing with the rest of her family. He still walked out the door.

The next day, to her heartbroken surprise, the sun still came up. The world was moving on and it was a school day. Still hoping it had all been a terrible dream from little sleep the night before, the 6th grader pleaded to stay in bed to no avail.

When it is time for her to get out of her mother's car to walk into school, she realizes she cannot do it. She blurts out that she just cannot go to school that day and probably not ever again for the rest of her life. Her mom, who must have been absolutely devastated herself, told her daughter that she could and she would.

The little girl screamed at her mom again, "I can't go to school. I'm too upset. I'll be crying all day and everyone will look at me and ask what is wrong. I am going to be the only 6th grade girl who has divorced parents. It's just too embarrassing and depressing. I don't even want to live! I sure don't care about school. I'm not getting out of the car!"

Her mother, as I recall, was a very wise woman and told her in a soft, firm voice saying these unforgettable words: "I know you are hurting. So am I, but you are not going to let this defeat you. You are not going to give up and quit living because of your father's bad choices. You are going to get out of this car, you are going to walk into your class, and you are going to make something out of yourself. You are NOT going to be messed up because you come from a divorced family. It's not an option!"

The little girl forced herself to get out of the car that day, knowing for sure she had the meanest, most heartless mother in the world. But somehow, she made it into her classroom that day followed by the next, and the next, and the next.

The last I heard of her she was a born-again Christian and gave God the credit for all He had done in her life, a life she never thought possible in the 6th grade. A life that in elementary school looked hopeless with such a dismal beginning.

I only thanked my mother a year ago for making me get out of the car and go to school that day. You will never know the well-chosen, healing words you can say to your child that will motivate their day and revolutionize their entire life. The opportunity is yours.

Box Talks

Journal Time

1. Did you have a medical kit in your toy box? If so, who did you treat most of the time? Your dolls, teddy bears, friends, and family pet? What was your motivation?

2. Which medical device and its metaphor did you relate to the most from this chapter? Write out why.

3. We all have some pain in our past that needs healing. Write what hurt came to mind when you read this chapter. Have you brought this pain before God? How can you begin to pursue healing?

Family Time

1. Write each family member a creative letter describing several things that you appreciate admire, and love about each other. Yes, siblings write letters to siblings. It won't kill them but may hurt a little.

2. Throughout the week send a text message, leave a post-it-note, or write a card just saying something positive.

3. Leave a note on your family member's pillow thanking him or her for something specific.

Epilogue

S EVERAL YEARS AGO, I was conducting a seminar about children and self-esteem. When I got home I was telling my husband about the points I covered in my speech. He began telling me, "Maybe we are making our kids feel *too* good about themselves. We don't want them to think they have no limitations. That is not reality." I told him he had made a valid point and I would give it some thought.

The very next morning while cleaning off the breakfast table, I was carrying a cereal bowl full of milk and uneaten cereal when the sleeve of my robe caught on the top of the chair. I trip in a stumbling, bumbling style. Amazingly however, I do not spill a drop from the bowl.

Relieved at my good fortune, I then say, "Oh thank you God."

My 5-year-old promptly replied, "You're welcome!"—Now that was a child who may have been feeling a little too good about himself at the moment. In all seriousness, with the exception of being so full of yourself that you think you *are* God, you really cannot have an overabundance of healthy self-esteem.

❖   ❖   ❖

With your new tools and skills you have the ability to implement and cement new ways of building self-esteem in your child. You've probably already been putting some of these new concepts into practice if you've worked through the BOX TALKS of each chapter. This book has either been new material for you to positively impact your children, or it's been a refresher course on how to motivate yourself toward success minded parenting.

You've been challenged and you are up for the challenge. It is exciting to think that you possess the creativity and ability to make a defined difference in your child or teen's self-esteem.

It is really about being cognizant of doing what needs to be done as a parent. There can be no more procrastination.

Getting Extra Credit

You care so much about your child that you are ready to do hard parenting. No matter what it takes you have everything necessary to make vital changes in your child's development. Breaking unhealthy patterns will not be as difficult as you may think. Even if you are doing an A+ parenting job, it's still nice to get the extra credit with some possible ideas you've learned.

Let's review what you've just read in this book. You are driving your family toward a positive and perhaps different destination. You will get there, even if you occasionally get lost.

Reducing the Rescue

You only rescue animals now, not children who are trying to manipulate. You are available when your kids need you, but not necessarily in ways that you have been in the past. You are willing to parent differently if it means a better future for your kids.

Hopefully you are now relieved to pick which battles you choose to have with your children. It gets very tiring to be in constant conflict but when necessary, you will do whatever it takes. Deciding what is important to address becomes easier each time you do it.

No one can be reminded often enough about the value of apologizing and making amends. This is so crucial for every member of the family. It blends into every relationship you have, even beyond your family.

Role Model for the Fashion Show

Every reader has to be improving what you mirror to your children. Once you learn the importance in this area, you become very aware of how you can role model your child toward success and healthy self-esteem.

Hopefully you learned some new ways to have fun and enjoy life more with your children. You don't have to use my ideas, but you will have more positive times with your children and teens if you learn to lighten up and laugh.

Dream and Listen

Learning to listen to the dreams of your kids is something very easy to implement. Being more positive, more accepting, and less judgmental will create better communication with those you love. You can see self-esteem growing before your very eyes.

The thing parents enjoy doing more than anything else is encouraging and cheering on their children. It is rewarding for both parents and kids. We just need reminders to do it more often. The results can be readily seen.

Directing the Journey

You've now been trained on how to train your child. You wear the conductor's hat. You are directing your child's life and development. Enjoy the journey.

The Blessing

You are most likely doing what you've learned to protect, nourish, challenge, and help your child to develop healthy self-esteem. Having positive self-esteem is a gift you are blessing your child with every day and hopefully you are feeling better about yourself along the way. It has been my honor to help you open the box of your child's self-esteem!

About the Author

PAMELA J. BOLEN is a Licensed Professional Counselor, Licensed Marriage and Family Therapist, Board Certified Clinical Hypnotherapist, and Certified Mental Health Service Provider in the field of Sports Counseling all in the state of Texas. Pamela is a popular speaker at churches, school districts, and corporate events. She has a B.S. degree in Psychology and a M.A. Psychology degree in Marriage and Family Therapy. She is married and has 3 children. They live in the Dallas/ Ft. Worth area.

End Notes

1 Noble, Perry. *Unleash!* Carol Stream, IL: Tyndale. 2012. Page 49.

2 Thompson, Janet. Praying For Your Prodigal Daughter. Monroe, LA: Howard. 2007. Page 44.

3 Chandler, Matt. *The Explicit Gospel.* Wheaton, IL: Crossway. 2012. Page 49.

4 Cloud, Dr. Henry and Dr. John Townsend. *Boundaries with Kids.* Grand Rapids, MI: Zondervan. 1998. Page 45.

5 Oliver, Gary and Carrie. *Raising Sons and Loving It!* Grand Rapids, MI: Zondervan. 2000. Pages 228–229.

6 *The Power Of A Praying Parent,* Stormie Omartian. Page 179.

7   Meyer, Joyce and Todd Hafer, *Battlefield of the Mind for Teens*. New York: NY: Warner Faith. 2006. Page 33.

8   www.selfhelpdaily.com/quotes-about-problems

9   http://www.brainyquote.com/quotes/quotes/f/friedrichn106364.html

10 http://science.howstuffworks.com/life/inside-the-mind/emotions/laughter7.htm

11 Hall, Ron and Denver Moore and Lynn Vincent. *Same Kind of Different as Me*. Nashville, TN: W. Publishing Group. 2006. Page 18.

12 Frost, Jo. *Supernanny*. New York, NY: Hyperion. 2005. Page 86.

13 "Derailed train in Arlington was hauling hazardous cargo" By Susan Schrock. http://www.star-telegram.com/2012/03/02/3780032/derailed-train-was-hauling-hazardous.html#storylink=cpy

14 Andy Andrews, First Conference, Gateway Church, January 9, 2013 http://gatewaypeople.com/sermons/150936

15 Leman, Dr. Kevin. *Have a New Kid by Friday*. Grand Rapids, MI: Revell. 2006. Page 27.

16 Ladd, Karol and Grace and Joy Ladd. *The Power of a Positive Teen*. Monroe, LA: Howard. 2005. Page 11.

17 Ortberg, John. *Everybody's Normal Till You Get to Know Them*. Grand Rapids, MI: Zondervan. 2003. Page 15.

www.ingramcontent.com/pod-product-compliance
Lightning Source LLC
Chambersburg PA
CBHW051423090426
42737CB00014B/2804